FROM POSITIVISM TO INTERPRETIVISM AND BEYOND

◆

*Tales of Transformation
in Educational and Social Research*

◆

(THE MIND-BODY CONNECTION)

FROM POSITIVISM TO INTERPRETIVISM AND BEYOND

◆

Tales of Transformation
in Educational and Social Research

◆

(THE MIND-BODY CONNECTION)

EDITED BY
Lous Heshusius AND **Keith Ballard**

WITH CONTRIBUTIONS BY:
James P. Anglin, Curt Dudley-Marling, Deborah J. Gallagher,
Egon G. Guba, Neita Kay Israelite, Mary Simpson Poplin,
William C. Rhodes, Thomas A. Schwandt, John K. Smith

FOREWORD BY ELLIOT W. EISNER

Teachers College, Columbia University
New York and London

Published by Teachers College Press, 1234 Amsterdam Avenue, New York, NY 10027

Library of Congress Cataloging-in-Publication Data

From positivism to interpretivism and beyond : tales of transformation
  in educational and social research (the mind-body connection) /
  edited by Lous Heshusius and Keith Ballard ; with contributions by
  James P. Anglin . . . [et al.].
     p. cm.
  Includes bibliographical references and index.
  ISBN 0-8077-3534-5 (cloth)
    1. Education — Research — Philosophy. 2. Social sciences — Research —
Philosophy. 3. Knowledge, Theory of. 4. Mind and body.
I. Heshusius, Lous. II. Ballard, Keith.
LB1028.F75   1996
370'.78 — dc20   96-14142

ISBN 0-8077-3534-5 (cloth)

Printed on acid-free paper
Manufactured in the United States of America

03 02 01 00 99 98 97 96   8 7 6 5 4 3 2 1

Contents

v

Foreword

From Positivism to Interpretivism and Beyond displays a feature rarely found in books addressing educational or social research: a congruence of form and content. By *congruence* I mean a fit between the message that the authors intend to send and the forms they use to send it. The dominant message—the theme of this book—is the embodied form of personal experience that is an inevitable but seldom-examined part of the process of doing educational and social research. We seldom reveal how we, as researchers, feel about what we are up to, or how those feelings shape our perceptions, alter our values, and enable us to construct meaning out of experience. We seldom share with others our own uncertainties about our work. We seldom reveal the sources of our discomfort with what we have been socialized to accept as legitimate procedures and defensible assumptions about what research entails—even when those procedures and assumptions gnaw upon us.

The reasons for the absence of such revelations seem quite clear. Objective social science, whether in the field of education or elsewhere, has little place for what is personal. What is personal is regarded as subjective, and what is subjective is both particular and unreliable; no science can be constructed on such seemingly unstable foundations. As a result, we have tried to function, by and large, as if our methods, our theories, our interpretive frameworks possess an objective neutrality, and we work up our reports, until recently at least, as if our intellectual thumbprints were not upon them. Replicability is a desideratum that tacitly suggests that the individual's contribution to the work cannot be so important that others are unable to replicate the research. We are to create procedures that will make it possible for others to mirror the work we create. In the process, individuality is lost.

There are, of course, virtues to replication, but it surely is not the whole story nor the only important virtue in efforts to shed light on things that matter. Knowing is not always dispassionate, and it is always personal. Its forms are rooted in feeling as well as in the cool light of reason. Knowing is embodied and having a sense of rightness, a nose for fit, a feeling of coherence matters. Indeed, the neglect of such qualities has been a source of distress so large for many of the authors of chapters

Coming out of the positivistic closet [handwritten annotation]

[handwritten annotation in left margin: *Add past to bio / college & grad sch*]

in this book that they have looked elsewhere for approaches more congruent with their intuitions. Body knowledge played a large part in the move from a constrained conception of rational science to a broader, more pluralistic conception of how research might be undertaken. *From Positivism to Interpretivism and Beyond* gives us an intimate glimpse into the personal side of educational and social research, a side that has been given little place in scholarly articles and books and few opportunities to emerge in professional meetings. Our research tradition has been one that denies the body, marginalizes emotion, and neutralizes values in its traditional technical approach to science. What we have here, in a sense, is a collection of confessions—or, if not confessions, revelations. These researchers are making their innards public.

One might well ask why anyone would be interested in inspecting the personal lives of people who changed their minds about the assumptions and methods employed in traditional research paradigms. I think the reasons are compelling. We are interested in the lives of others because their lives, filled as they are with discomforts, uncertainties, frustrations, and doubts, also reflect our own feelings about aspects of our scholarly life. To be sure, there are some who are certain about what they are doing and have done, who are confident that the assumptions they make about the "discovery" of knowledge are true. But increasingly the door to doubt has been widened; today more of us are less sure that mechanistic, positivistic, or neopositivistic assumptions about knowledge are appropriate in any scientific domain, but especially those that address human beings. The presence of a volume that helps scholars come out of the positivistic closet does so because it shows that coming out is possible, that you can survive if you do, and that there are others who share your doubts and uncertainties. *From Positivism to Interpretivism and Beyond* acknowledges what has been denied and suppressed. In so doing, it humanizes the research process.

To reveal so personal a feature of scholarly life requires a form that makes such revelation possible; enter narrative. The story, a tale told over time, has the capacity to display intimacies. In the essays that constitute the chapters of this book, stories unfold. We gain access to personal moments because these moments of change, of doubt, of discomfort are woven into real tales about real people in real situations. The result is no analytical or formal display of data, no excursion into theoretical abstractions, but rather a personal biographical narrative; the authors whom you will read are willing to allow us into their lives. What we find in the stories they tell have both common and unique features. What is common is the shared recognition that mechanistic science did not fit their worldview. The experience that these authors knew in their own professional socialization as graduate students and, for others, as full-fledged academics was not congruent with their basic intuitions. And they had the courage to look for alternatives. That sequence of discomfort and search is what all of the authors share. What differs among them are the sources of their feelings. For some the motivation is rooted in an internal, almost physical experience. For others, it is more cerebral, an inability to reason about what itself might not yield to the constraints of reason. These differences in the sources of the shift or attraction to bodily based research, or narrative orientation to inquiry or naturalistic approaches, or more broadly, qualitative approaches — there is no single term to cover them all — also leads to two other conflicting views about the appropriateness of positivism as a prototypical methodological paradigm for research on humans. One view regards it as useful, insofar as it is but one of many ways in which legitimate inquiry can go forward. This view is pluralistic in character. Another view holds that even pluralism has no place for a fundamentally wrongheaded approach to research. Positivism simply has no legitimate function in the world of research methods because it distorts by both commission and omission. The controversy between these views is likely to continue. No resolution is found in this book. Perhaps that is as it should be. Open-endedness and differential perspective belong in its orientation to knowing.

It is significant that a book of this kind should appear at all. It is reassuring that it has. It signifies that there is support for the public display of our most personal moments. Such a display depends upon trust; vulnerability cannot be courted unless there is a sense of safety. Safety depends upon the belief that it is okay with others to say what is on your mind or in your heart. The field of educational and social research has indeed changed, and this volume is both a marker and a stimulus to further change.

But the future of the general orientation to research reflected in this book cannot rest solely upon the confessions of researchers telling stories about their personal lives. It must be based upon the quality of the light that new research methods provide. These methods must finally be tested in the quality of the work they yield. Personal testimony can go only so far. The proof, as they say, is in the pudding. We live in yeasty times. *From Positivism to Interpretivism and Beyond* contributes significantly to the growing legitimation of other ways of seeing things. We *do* need binocular vision. It is the only way to achieve depth of field. It is to the credit of the editors and authors that they have contributed to its achievement.

Elliot W. Eisner
Stanford University

Preface

The roots of this book go back a long way to experiences in our academic and professional lives that required us to repress the somatic and emotive dimensions of knowing. Becoming aware that others felt much the same way, we slowly became convinced that these experiences needed to be told.

The central focus of this book, then, is on bodily and emotive ways of knowing. To bring out these dimensions in the academic world, we needed a story around which to fashion their significance. We decided to focus on the shift from a positivist to an interpretive, qualitative apprehension of research, a shift that many have gone through and a shift, we thought, so deep and radical that it would have had to be accompanied, as in our own case, by impulses of deep visceral, somatic, and emotive knowing.

Several of the contributors to this book told us that their participation had been uniquely important to them, enabling them to address dimensions of scholarship that they knew to be important and that graduate students in particular had often asked them about, but which they had not been able to discuss in any formal way. We had asked our colleagues to be as personal as they wished to be, and we have been struck by—and grateful for—the honesty and directness that characterize all contributions. Several contributors noted delight in being asked to write as themselves, while some said in addition that publishing their stories made them just a little uneasy. We offered of course to delete anything they had written, and would respectfully have accepted withdrawal of their piece if they had so wished, but that was not their desire. Their unease was accepted almost happily as a byproduct of doing something that was impossible to do under traditional positivist rules, and something that becomes difficult in general when one grows up: telling what is perceived as truth without deliberately leaving out entire dimensions of experience.

We had three criteria for selecting contributors. We sought colleagues who had been trained in a positivist set of beliefs and had later taken an interpretivist, qualitative turn; a combination of some who had spent many years in the academic world as well as some who were relatively new to it; and colleagues who covered a wide range of interests within education. With regard to the latter, contributors work in the areas of teacher education, educational evaluation, education of the deaf, literacy acquisition, feminist thought, disability advocacy and research, youth care and family education, history and philosophy of education, and special education. The contributors come from white, Anglo-Saxon, heterosexual, and able-bodied backgrounds. Personal accounts by scholars of different color, ethnicity, sexual orientation, and physical sensory or other abilities would undoubtedly have broadened the complexity of somatic and emotive knowing, but this was not achieved in this work.

In Chapter 1 we address the significance of the tacit, somatic, and emotive sources of knowing, drawing from interdisciplinary literature. We also explain how the contributors were asked to write about the events and emotions associated with changing their fundamental beliefs about what it means to do research. Their accounts comprise Chapter 2 of the book. In Chapter 3 contributors reflect on each other's stories and say what they would wish the future of educational and social research to be 50 years from now, if it were up to them. In the final chapter we note parameters of this kind of work, and some issues and questions left for further exploration.

We believe we speak to a wide range of readers: colleagues and students who may find within these stories experiences and emotions that resonate with their own and who may find support for their sense that personal ways of knowing are central to inquiry. Given the paradigmatic focus of the book, it is equally relevant for those in fields of social inquiry other than education.

We thank the University of Otago, New Zealand for the grant from the William Evans Visiting Fellowship Fund that made it possible for us to work together in Dunedin. We thank Mildred Jaeger, York University, Toronto, and Christine Gardener, University of Otago, for their expert assistance in preparing the manuscript. And we thank Brian Ellerbeck, our editor at Teachers College Press, for his receptivity to and interest in how we see the world and our place as academics in it.

FROM POSITIVISM TO INTERPRETIVISM AND BEYOND

◆

*Tales of Transformation
in Educational and Social Research*

◆

(The Mind-Body Connection)

1

How Do We Count the Ways We Know? Some Background to the Project

Lous Heshusius and Keith Ballard

> *Teacher*: Good try, Colin. You're doing really well.
> *Colin*: Don't say that.
> *Teacher*: Why not?
> *Colin*: Because.
> *Teacher*: Because why?
> *Colin*: Because my stomach doesn't think so, that's why (pointing to his stomach).
> (Crown, 1990)

> The heart has its reasons of which reason knows nothing: we know this in a thousand ways.
> Blaise Pascal

For many of us, there are moments in our professional development, as in the whole of life, when we know that we no longer believe what we had long accepted as true and correct. Something no longer feels right: It is a feeling that arises in our deeper psyche, in our somatic-emotional life. Often, this feeling is dismissed at the academic-intellectual level and work continues as usual in the familiar ways in which our profession has socialized us. For some, however, the confrontation can become so bothersome, and the need to trust one's inner knowing so strong, that the felt discomfort leads to an intense intellectual analysis.

It is often only in retrospect that we can articulate the initial feelings. Even then, most of us keep such reflection to ourselves or share it only informally with friendly colleagues. It rarely enters the professional literature, which typically acknowledges only abstract and intellectualized modes of knowing and of discourse. As historian of science Morris Berman (1989, p. 131) aptly comments, we have only analytic methodologies, not methodologies of feeling and sensing.

 In this book we explore modes of awareness and modes of knowing that some educational thinkers experienced when changing from a quantitative, positivist epistemological framework to a qualitative, interpretive one.[1] It is a shift that involves a fundamental deconstruction and reconstruction of agreements about what counts as real and how we allow each other to claim knowledge. We would like to stress that the paradigmatic shift itself was not the substantive concern when we started to think of writing this book. It simply offered itself as a fine story around which to illustrate the role somatic knowing plays in intellectual work. In other words, we could just as easily have chosen a different story. We selected this one because it lent itself so well to the task, as the shift it reflects is so radical that it was bound to have involved considerable somatic and emotive input.

The idea for the book emerged from our own experiences, and we add the particulars of our stories to those of our colleagues. When we started to consciously reflect on how we had changed our most basic beliefs, we had to acknowledge that we knew, before we could account for it intellectually, that we no longer believed in what we were doing or in what we were being taught. That is, while the dominant assumptions still made sense rationally in terms of how things are done, they no longer made sense somatically and affectively. Something *felt* wrong. Our bodies told us so. For both of us, the conscious shift in paradigmatic assumptions was initially not brought about by a systematically carried out intellectual pursuit. Rather, the impetus for this transformation was events and incidents that involved modes of awareness that were distinctly somatic and affective. These occasions and the values and reactions they engendered placed us in confrontation with our academic and professional commitments. As we tried to trace the origins of this clash in fundamental epistemological assumptions, it became overwhelmingly clear to us that somatic and affective modes of awareness came prior to and informed changes at the intellectual level.

Embodied and Disembodied Knowing

Children still know in an embodied way, relying on their somatic and affective knowing as a primary source of information. Penny Oldfather (1991, p. 181) spent a year in a 5th grade classroom listening to children talk about what turns them on or turns them off in their learning. The following conversation occurred when she asked a student how he felt when he was asked by his teacher to do something he could not do or disliked doing.

Joe: My whole body feels like I want to throw up or something if I don't like something.
Researcher: Do you go ahead and do it?
Joe: Sometimes I just break down, really . . .
Researcher: So you sort of don't do it, basically?
Joe: I can't do it if I . . . I can't do it at all.
Researcher: When you say you break down, how do you mean? What happens?
Joe: I mean I feel sick . . . my body feels completely wrong.

The quote taken from Louise Crown (1990) at the beginning of this chapter is from an interchange with a young student in which she had presented him with a series of unrelated one-syllable words, one at a time. Colin, the student, had been asked to correctly identify the final sound of each word. Colin was working hard but struggling with this task. As the result of an attempt to at least reward his effort, the exchange noted in the quote occurred. Colin's stomach knew better than the researcher's rational-methodological mode of knowing.

It is anybody's guess as to how many of us, students, teachers, and educational researchers, walk around in schools and universities with feelings of bodily and emotional stress because of the disembodiment involved in how we are taught to teach, to learn, and to do research. Probably there are hordes of us. As we become adults, we learn how to repress somatic awareness, and many of us can no longer tell when our stomachs know better than our minds, when our bodies feel completely wrong, or why we develop headaches. We cover up the stress caused by the disembodiment of our work by still more work, or by still another cup of coffee. Lack of meaning, which points, by definition, to the loss of a participatory mode of knowing, to lack of somatic and emotional involvement (see Berman, 1989; Johnson, 1983, Tarnas, 1991), is no longer accurately felt, understood, and acted on.

With adulthood and professional training, we learn to separate what has come to be seen as rational ways of knowing from nonrational ones, to separate disembodied ways of knowing from embodied ones, assigning an epistemologically privileged status to the former. We are so used to drawing this separation that we assume it has always been that way. As Morris Berman (1984, p. 10) states, however:

> For more than 99 percent of human history, the world was enchanted and man (sic) saw himself as an integral part of it. The complete reversal of this perception in a mere four hundred years or so has destroyed the continuity of human experience and the integrity of the human psyche. It has very nearly wrecked the planet as well. The only hope, or so it seems to me, is the re-enchantment of the world.

Until quite recently, then, the very act of affective and somatic participation *was* knowing. Elsewhere, Berman (1989, p. 111) goes on to say: "'the facts' were first and foremost what happened on a psychic, and emotional level; indeed, if this got left out, it was fair to say that *nothing happened*." The essential truth was an interior one. To omit this was to give the reader, or the listener, no significant information whatsoever. However, in the transition to modernity (meaning here the time period from the Scientific Revolution to the present), the significance of interior knowing was severed: an enchanted understanding of world and self became a disenchanted one. From then on, it was necessary to place oneself in a detached, nonparticipatory relation to that which one wanted to know, including toward oneself. The knower was no longer allowed to be enchanted in the act of knowing, that is, to fully participate at the spiritual, psychological, emotional, and somatic levels. In clarifying the term "enchanted," David Griffin (1988, p. 12) notes, "an *enchanted science* is a wholly different thing from a *sacred science*; in fact, the decline of the latter is necessary for the reemergence of the former." The concept of science resulting from the Scientific Revolution is one of a sacred science, a science whose methods and worldview are thought to be immune from social and personal influences. Such disenchanted, sacred science needs to be "desacralized," to use Griffin's phrase, if we are again to be able to think of knowing as participatory, involving the whole of life.

The metaphors and worldview that emerged from the rise of Western science demand that we believe in the possibility of separating fact from value, mind from body, mind from emotion, and self from other. With its emphasis on scientific, methodological, and quantitative rationality, Western thought began to liquidate all other ways of knowing:

not intuition; not imagination; not feelings; not spiritual knowing; not knowing through connecting, participation, and identification; not qualitative subtleties; and surely not the knowledge that the body holds. Only the elegant, well-controlled cleanliness of mathematical certainty could count as knowledge. Descartes's "*Cogito, ergo sum*" has worked itself into virtually all niches of our lives. Detailed accounts of how and for what ideological reasons this process of severance occurred are amply available. Patriarchal and technological motives involving fear and distrust of the body, of the senses, of emotions, of femaleness all played a central role (see, e.g., Berman, 1984, 1989; Bordo, 1986, 1987; Griffin, 1988; E. F. Keller, 1985; C. Keller, 1988; Kubrin, 1981; Prigogine & Stengers, 1984; Rose, 1994; Tarnas, 1991). In Jagger's (1989, p. 145) words, not only has reason been contrasted with emotion, but it has also been associated with the mental, the cultural, the universal, the public, and the male, in other words, with members of the dominant political and cultural groups, whereas emotion has been associated with the irrational, the physical, the natural, the particular, the private, and, of course, the female and non-white racial groups. Some have indeed proposed that the separation between reason and emotion is itself a Euroamerican cultural construction and a master symbol, Jagger further notes (p. 147). In Western thought, emotive as well as somatic life have been subversive of knowledge.

Somatic and emotional knowing, then, came to be regarded as unreliable, biased, and "only" subjective, a mode of knowing that may be useful for our intimate, personal lives, but not for claiming knowledge about the world. Many people, particularly in intellectual settings such as the academic world, would still agree with this view. Such agreement is part of a culturally conditioned process. Prior to the Scientific Revolution, *lack* of identification through the somatic and affective modes of knowing was regarded as strange and unreliable (Berman, 1989, pp. 112–113; see also Griffin, 1988; Keller, 1985). None of this is to deny the importance of reason and rationality. They are of course indispensable. The problem of rationality and reason is historical and ideological. Forms of scientific rationality and reasoning look for evidence exclusively in material reality and in abstraction. Somatic-emotive knowing seeks evidence in nonmaterial reality. One could perhaps think of somatic-emotive knowing as a different form of rationality, distinguishing it from irrationality.

Interior knowing cannot be intellectually refuted; it is invisible and lives throughout our being. Michael Polanyi (1966) wrote his now-classic analysis of tacit knowledge, the knowing that we know but cannot tell because it is initially visceral and internal. He points to passion and "personal obsession," which guide us in our quest for knowledge. The manner in which we come to understand something is "strictly personal," says Polanyi (1966, pp. 75–76). We "extend our body to include (what we come to know) so that we come to dwell in it" (Polanyi, 1966, p. 16). Bodily knowing, or "indwelling," says Polanyi, is central to all acts of knowing. Ernest Schachtel (1959, p. 225) has rendered a psychological analysis of what he calls "allocentric knowing" (as contrasted to autocentric knowing), a knowing that is concerned with both the totality of that which one wants to come to understand, and with the "participation of the total person." The participation of the total person constitutes a "*total turning to it*," to that which one wants to come to know. It is an attitude, he says, of profound interest and complete openness. It results in knowing that is not preshaped by a separation of the rational from the nonrational.

Nobel Laureate Barbara McClintock, who studied the manner in which genetic forces in corn plants interact with the whole organism, stressed over and over the importance of "inner knowing." Willis Harman (1988) observes that McClintock is perhaps the most lucid of all writers on the somatic-affective nature of her involvement in science. She is "one of the rare scientists who has stated openly what others have confessed secretly" (Harman, 1988, p. 16). Evelyn Fox Keller (1983, pp. 197–198) characterizes McClintock's scientific vocabulary as one of empathy, affection, love, and kinship. Above all, McClintock used to say, one must have "a feeling for the organism." She always trusted her feeling that she knew, although she could not yet tell, and called it knowing in "a complete internal way" (Keller, 1983, p. 203).

Interior knowing cannot be intellectually refuted, but it can be intellectually rejected, which is precisely what happened as a result of the Scientific Revolution. As Morris Berman (1989, p. 113) notes, it is important to observe that the intellectual rejection of inner knowing did *not* mean that affective and somatic knowing became truly repressed or rejected, only that one particular emotion reigned over all others, namely, the emotional need to think of oneself as objective. It is a very definite emotion, one that Berman describes as the craving for psychological and existential security, a security that appeared to be obtainable by creating a system of beliefs that held that nature could be securely controlled. Establishing such beliefs was accomplished by positing the possibility of a detached, disenchanted, and disembodied relation to nature, to other, and to the self, a relation brought about by conceptualizing the knower as separate from and superior to the known. Evelyn Fox Keller (1985, p. 70) likewise observes that the dream of objectivity contained precisely what it rejects: "the vivid traces of a reflected self image." It is the investment in impersonality, Keller states, the claim to have escaped the influence of desires, wishes, and beliefs, that constitutes the bravura of modern man, and at the same time reveals his peculiar subjectivity.

As a result of this disenchanted, disembodied stance toward both ontology and epistemology, the idea of mastery of and control over nature could be articulated. As Ilya Prigogine and Isabelle Stengers (1984, p. 32) comment, a disenchanted world is a world liable to control and manipulation: "man, a stranger to the world, sets himself up as its master." What made the project of disembodiment seem possible, then, was the idea that reliable knowledge could only be obtained through externalizing modes of knowing, through distancing, quantification, atomization, manipulation, and experimentation. This scientific rationality purported to shield us from direct, psychic, emotional, somatic participation in that which we want to come to know. It purported to shield us even from direct, psychic, and somatic participation in knowing ourselves.

Some efforts at reconstructing epistemologies focus on the significance of inner ways of knowing. In his book *Coming to Our Senses: Body and Spirit in the Hidden History of the West*, Morris Berman (1989) rewrites Western history from the perspective of collective somatic life. Ever since the rise of Western science, he concludes, we have lost our senses in the way we approach knowledge of nature, of others, and of ourselves. And to loose your senses, to leave your body behind and believe you still can know anything at all, "is quite literally a form of madness" (Berman, 1989, p. 110).

Don Johnson (1983, pp. 22–23) describes the loss of somatic knowing in direct relation to the ways we live our day-to-day lives. He amply illustrates how we come to manifest the mind-body and mind-emotion split that mirrors the nature of Western science itself. Johnson reminds us that the worldview that ensued from Descartes's dualisms carries its own logical conclusion: since I do not have immediate contact with any of the realities of my ordinary life, I can be deluded about any of them. The only thing I can be sure about is that I can think: I cannot be sure about intuition, love, or bodily or spiritual knowing as valid ways to know. Even about my body, my health, and my emotions, I can have reliable knowledge only through the formalized methods of science. Berman (1989) and Johnson (1983) document how the formalized separation of mind from body and from emotion has manifested itself in many areas in life, including the way we relate (or do not relate) to animals and to the ecological environment, the way many of us have been born in sterile hospitals, the alienating ways children are taught in school, the way we project our alienation and distrust of our own bodies onto those whose bodies are different from ours, and in modern warfare, where the enemy, en masse and from a distance, is disembodied, that is, made faceless and anonymous before they are killed. Here, the self–other connection has become completely nonexistent: "Accustomed to our own disembodiment", says Johnson (1983, p. 116), "we don't even have to think of the enemy as embodied."

Within social work, Dennis Saleebey (1992) laments the loss of the significance of the body. Social work has snubbed bodily knowing, as it has been influenced by the hegemony of science in its rational/technological orientation. What social work needs to do, Saleebey says, is work toward an integration of mind and body nestled more firmly within social contexts. This would mean, among other things, helping clients to regain a sense of their somatic lives and to listen to the knowledge of their bodies as a guide to what to do. It would mean that social workers must become more receptive so they can tune into the subtle shifts in somatic expression in their clients to better understand them. This would require social workers to become more aware of bodily presence, including their own. It would involve blurring the boundaries between body and mind, and body and consciousness. The willingness to deliberately do so is crucial. Holistic health, yoga, and other forms of body-mind connectedness can further enable the expansion of one's experience of one's own bodily knowing, and heighten awareness of the nonverbal knowing of others. As Philipa Rothfield (1990, p. 139) notes, this contradicts the modern belief that the body is neutral and passive with regard to consciousness and the construction of knowledge. Instead, blurring the boundaries between body and mind helps the development of a "mindful body" (Rothfield, 1990, p. 139). A mindful body has no place in modernity's understanding of knowledge construction. Nor, for that matter, does an "embodied mind" (Varela, Thompson, & Rosch, 1993). Both a mindful body and an embodied mind are needed to tap into somatic and emotive sources of knowing.

The need to return to one's bodily-emotional grounding, if we are to heal from the alienating effects of Cartesian dualisms, is a strong message in contemporary thought. As we are struggling to regather the kind of knowing that involves the whole of life, we can see the positivist tradition as an epistemology that deemed itself more clever than life itself. We are borrowing the theme of deeming itself "more clever than life itself" from Vaclav Havel's (1992b, pp. 62–63) eloquent plea for the embodiment of political life, for the need for today's politician to be in touch again with her/his own deep subjectivity and somatic knowing as the most vital link to others (see also Havel, 1992a).

Across disciplines, then, as in many areas of practical life, many are, often desperately, searching for a way back to ourselves, back to experiencing ourselves and others (human or nonhuman) as whole again, lest we suffocate even to greater and more unbearable degrees than we already have, from the alienating, disenchanted consciousness inherent in positivist and mechanistic traditions.

Overcoming Cartesian Dualisms

Within contemporary thought, major attempts have been made to critique and go beyond Cartesian dualisms. It does not appear, however, that these efforts have been successful at integrating body-mind-emotion in conceptualizations of both knowledge *and* modes of discourse. Apart from the move from positivist to interpretivist thought, there are at least two other movements that should be noted. The purpose here is not to attempt comprehensive accounts or critiques, but to provide a context for our view that the attempts at (re)uniting internal and external, rational and nonrational ways of knowing turn out to be a far more difficult undertaking than we might have imagined.

Postmodern deconstructionist thought demystifies Cartesian dualisms in that it claims the impossibility of modernity's belief in representation. Recognizing that the use of the words *postmodern* and *deconstructionism* are widespread and their meanings varied, we use the terms here in what seems to be the most common meaning given to them in North American social science literature. As such, postmodern deconstructionist thought points to the impossibility of describing reality through a transparent language, a reality that was supposedly "out there," separate from us. An objective reality does not exist because there is no extralinguistic referent, and therefore, language being a symbolic system, there is nothing beyond the symbolic system to which a text can refer. Therefore, there can never be an authentic statement from one person to another about anything in any objective sense. Reality is seen as text, endlessly interpretable—and therefore deconstructable—through language, never "true" in itself. Language is seen as a system of power relations rather than a transparent medium. Textuality becomes the primary "reality" of life, of the world, and of subjects (that is, of socially constructed identities): Reality itself has become a text and cannot be more than a text.

What is important for our discussion is the apparent dismissal in deconstructionist thought of inner mind-body and mind-emotion connectedness as a way of knowing outside of language. Language is seen as the essential tool, as the bottom line. In the end, there is only a system of linguistic structures. [2]

Deconstructionist discourse has been characterized as highly abstract and highly rational. For many, it is not a mode of discourse in which body, emotions, mind, and experience unite. The discourse is difficult to access, and has been characterized by some as nihilistic and reactionary (e.g., as noted in Lather, 1991; see also Anderson, 1990; Tarnas, 1991; Waugh, 1989), representing still another version of disembodiment. The critics who refer to the hyperrationality of the discourse generally stop short of commenting on the need to connect body, mind, and emotion in ways of knowing and in modes of discourse. Exceptions to this include Morris Berman (1989), as well as Patricia Waugh (1989) who stresses, from a distinctly feminist perspective, the need to embody the postmodern discourse. Talking about the invalidity of the body-emotion-mind separation is not enough. As Berman (1989, p. 122), we believe, pegs it precisely, deconstructionist thought attempts to recover the Cartesian mind-body and value-fact split by making the journey, once more, within the mind only, thereby perpetuating the conceptual categories of the modern era: "Mind and body, fact and value, still wind up on opposite sides of the fence."

Cartesian conceptual dualisms may be far more deeply ingrained than we realize. If we wish to transform ourselves into an embodied existence, then the question becomes how to live in *and* talk about an embodied reality, how to foster, also in our modes of discourse (particularly in modes of discourse, given the powerful influence of language), an embodied reality that many long to live in.

Another major attempt to overcome the alienation suffered by Cartesian dualisms is holistic thought. The majority of educators who are using holistic principles to reconceptualize education depend on two major sources. They either rely primarily on the spiritual and humanistic traditions (see J. P. Miller, 1988; R. Miller, 1990), or they rely on the new sciences of complexity (see, e.g., Crowell, 1989; Doll, 1986, 1993; Heshusius, 1989, 1995; Rhodes, 1987; Sawada & Caley, 1985). Some depend on both (Kesson, 1991; Oliver & Gershman, 1989; Sloan, 1984). Several authors refer to their framework as the "new paradigm" in which the search for wholeness is crucial. In exploring what the new sciences of complexity have to offer to education, some educators use conceptual and abstract categories and language exclusively. Others do point to the importance of the inner, personal ways of knowing. Some refer particularly to the centrality of imagination and deep insight, while others stress the importance of real-life meaning and emotional engagement in any act of knowing. The general importance of the mind-body connection might be mentioned, but explicit emphasis on the body as a primary source of knowing is noted by only a few. Donald Oliver and Kathleen Gershman's (1989) concept of "Grounded Knowing" is perhaps most reflective of a conception of education that demands that the mind, the body, and the emotions be united. These publications, however, are typically written in the dominant rational mode of discourse, as if the knowing they contain was constructed exclusively by the reasoning process. This is not to say that rational discourse is not important. On the contrary, it is to say that in its exclusive use, it is incomplete and obscures and distorts the processes that give rise to knowledge claims.

In these attempts, then, toward "the recovery of wholeness," to borrow Sloan's (1984) phrase, the danger of continuing the old conceptual categories of the mind-body and mind-emotion separation has not necessarily disappeared. While the conceptual principles of holism (such as self-organization, self-regulation, emergent properties, the role of novelty, spontaneous transformation, complexity, and so forth) are enriching and consequential, with great power to get education out from under the mechanistic framework, the danger exists that through the mode of discourse used, we may once more become mired in rational thought and abstract categories removed from actual and inner experience. The construct of holism could become a disembodied holism, sterilized and abstracted, in both its content and its mode of discourse (see also Berman, 1989, pp. 305–307, who is particularly pessimistic in this regard). Holistic educational inquiry could end up leaving the real-life bodies and emotions of students and teachers by the wayside once more in its attempts at recovering a "wholeness" that is only conceptual and rational.

Knowing in Education

Increasingly, educators are analyzing the influence of the Western scientific mindset on education. In educational research, the assumptions that characterize the positivist, quantitative approach to research have been extensively documented, debated, argued, historicized, and otherwise demystified. Discussions have included the nature of the relationship between the concepts of fact and value, the concept of objectivity and subjectivity, the influence of the researcher's own needs, interests, and motivations, the problem of power inequalities, the nature of the relationship between the researcher and the researched, and the relationship between science and the humanities (Denzin & Lincoln, 1994a; Eisner & Peshkin, 1990; Guba, 1990). Tensions similar to those that underlie these discussions have also been addressed in other areas of education, such as curriculum inquiry (Doll, 1986, 1993; Sawada & Caley, 1985), special education (Ballard, 1987, 1995; Heshusius, 1989, 1995; Poplin, 1988; Skrtic, 1991), and literacy acquisition (Edelsky, 1990).

Typically, however, these critiques continue to be written in a mode of discourse that suggests that they are the result of an intellectual exercise only. Thus, while these critics point to the intricate and inextricable connection between value and fact and between the known and the knower, thereby disassociating themselves from Cartesian splits, the manner of discourse is, with a few exceptions, incommensurate with the argument that value and fact, knower and the known, are intricately related, and continues to reflect that very split. The danger in all this is that such intellectual analysis then appears to others, and in time to oneself, to be just that, an intellectual exercise. The analytical process is severed from the initial knowing that was embedded in the somatic-emotional dimensions of our lives. Dualistic thought has worked itself so deeply into our psyche that we have learned to ignore the real starting points of our understandings. We then proceed in our writing as if these understandings started in the head instead. "What," asks Berman (1989, p. 107), "if it turned out that most of what was in the history books, or even in the daily newspapers, had nothing to do with life as it was actually lived?" We believe the same question must be asked of accounts of educational realities and of the ways in which we report how these accounts come into being. Borrowing Elliott Eisner's (1993, p. 7) words, "our discourse defines neither the scope of our rationality nor the varieties of our understandings."

Stories of Change: Changing Stories

As we talked to colleagues and thought of our own experiences in shifting fundamental assumptions, it became more and more apparent that most of us knew somatically and emotionally before we knew intellectually that we needed to change our beliefs. Encounters or incidents in life, a deeply personal experience, run-ins with social and professional structures and with established practices, involvement in the arts, a bodily knowing that suddenly surges; all can trigger the somatic awareness that something is no longer right. While some had shared these realizations in private, they had not done so in professional journals or conference papers (with one or two exceptions). One does not do that. But we think we should. Otherwise we perpetuate in our professional lives the very mind-body and mind-emotion separation our intellectual

writings argue against. We would continue to perpetuate the very Cartesian dualisms we say we no longer believe in.

We therefore invited 10 colleagues to tell their story of how fundamental change in their paradigmatic beliefs came about. Some were people we knew well, some we had met once or twice, and some we knew
only through their work. Most had fully adhered to a positivist set of
assumptions and had subsequently shifted to an interpretivist perspective. The others, while never having fully bought into a positivist foundation, were confronted with it in their training and, finding it wanting,
deliberately set out to search for alternatives.

In our letter of invitation to participate, we identified the key issues
our project aimed to address, and asked our colleagues for their participation, which would have two parts. The first part would be the writing
of their inner story about the nature of their particular experience in
shifting fundamental assumptions from the past to the present. We
stressed that theirs was to be an inside story, a story of inner change. An
intellectual essay would not do. We then sent all of these stories to all
contributors to read, and asked them to each write a second chapter in
which they could reflect on the collective themes and issues raised in the
stories, and set out their wishes with regard to future developments. In
particular, we asked them to address what they would wish educational
research to look like 50 years from now, if it were up to them. We placed
an emphasis on *wishing*, as the act of wishing, more likely than of
thinking, guessing, or predicting, involves the somatic-emotive dimensions. We therefore did not ask, What do you think will have happened
to educational research 50 years from now? Rather, we asked, What
would you *wish* educational research to become in 50 years?

Of the 10 colleagues invited, 1 had to decline because of other
commitments. All reacted positively to the project. They saw the project
as "fun," "important," "very interesting," "overdue," and a chance to
publicly respond to questions similar to those that others (especially
graduate students) had asked them. Some of the contributors implied
that to write such a story sounded like a breeze, something they could do
in a day or two. As the stories will show, the process did not quite turn
out to be a breeze! For some it rather resembled a small hurricane,
calling up unexpected issues and questions, and unexpected difficulties
in turning inward to recount their own journeys toward interpretivist,
qualitative research.

In presenting these tales, then, we shift our attention from the formalized story of paradigmatic change in science, of which there now are
many, to the inner story of paradigmatic change in academics; that is,
their interior story that includes somatic-emotional knowing, our pri-

mary interest in this book. Not many stories such as these are made public, certainly not in education. We believe that their absence causes a distorted understanding of how human beings come to know.

A note of caution is in order, so that we will not be misunderstood. We would like to stress that we are not making the case for surface, subjective knowledge. We are not referring to surface feelings, to our predilections, likes, and dislikes, but to the layers of affective-somatic knowing that guide the deeper course of our intellectual lives. This is not to say that rational and technical forms of knowing do not deeply guide our lives as well. However, the latter have received ample attention and analysis in theories of knowledge. The former have mainly been the object of psychological study.

By somatic and affective modes of knowing, then, we are not referring to theoretical constructs such as the unconscious in its typical clinical sense. Instead, we refer to direct modes of knowing, to actual locations of primary knowledge, to primary sources of information. We are expressing the belief that forms of discourse need to be welcomed that no longer reflect the forced separation of what has come to be seen as interior and exterior modes of knowing. Knowledge, says physicist David Bohm (1984, p. 383) in his discussion on insights, values, and education, "is an *active process*, which is present not only in abstract thought, but which enters pervasively into desire, will, action, and indeed into the whole of life."

Before we can become more comfortable in expressing ourselves in an embodied mode of discourse, we must break through the Cartesian dictates that tell us to pretend that somatic, emotional knowing plays no explicit part in how we gain our insights. One way to do so, it seemed to us, was a full-fledged focus on interior ways of knowing. Hence this book. The stories and reflections contained in Chapters 2 and 3, then, are not meant to be a series of interesting and sometimes amusing accounts (although of course we hope you will find them interesting). They constitute an engagement in epistemology, more precisely, an engagement in an "epistemology of feeling" (Keller, 1988, p. 176).

The reader may say: I agree that somatic knowing is interesting, and that telling its tale deepens our understanding of the individual life of the researcher, but now what? What good does it really do? What can research accomplish differently and better if we explicitly attend to the somatic dimension of knowledge construction? We would respond in the following way to those who would pose these or similar questions.

To impose what are essentially means-ends challenges of evidence implies that somatic knowing is enclosed within the individual, that it is private, and that it has no consequences beyond the self. It assigns somatic knowing back to its repressed position. It implies that there is no intrinsic value in somatic knowing; that is, no value that is *simultaneously* present for the individual and for the world beyond the individual. It implies that its value for research has to be proven by phrasing it in the language of an instrumental rationality within which one can stipulate in a means-ends fashion what leads to what.

To further clarify the problem involved in submitting an evaluation of the importance of somatic-emotive knowing to challenges of evidence, it may be helpful to think of some analogies. For example, understanding the story of the environment has traditionally been phrased in a means-ends relationship (needed for our survival, for long-term economic benefit, etc.) because nature was not seen to have intrinsic value. Increasingly, nature's inherent value is understood in its intrinsic relation to all of life. Not that long ago, the female experience, by and large, had little intrinsic value. Its value lay in its subservient means-ends relationship to patriarchical needs, personal and institutional. To ask, Why focus on the female experience? It may be interesting, but what good does it do? would similarly have assigned women's experience back to its inferior status. We now know that the stories of nature, of femaleness, of indigenous life, and so forth *simultaneously* have private value and value beyond their own existence. Their previously denied intrinsic values have made themselves visible, over time, in description and elaboration. Somatic knowing, in our view, is an integral part of human knowing. It is one more repressed dimension of life that needs description and elaboration, not means-ends stipulations, to evince its significance.

In shifting fundamental assumptions, then, we are shifting stories. Many of us are no longer happy with the old but are not clear about the new; we are "in between stories," as the contemporary phrase goes. In this time of change and ambiguity, it is particularly important to pay careful attention to inner ways of knowing, to somatic and affective layers, so that we might consciously work on the evolution of our story. While inner ways of knowing cannot be the sole source of knowledge, they are a major source of knowledge. We must therefore acknowledge, and do so publicly, that the formulation of a different story is not exclusively an intellectual affair. For many, as the stories in Chapter 2 show, it issues equally, or even primarily, from the belly and the heart.

Notes

1. We use the term *positivism* here in the broad sense, referring to the doctrine that science is the positive, that is, the true knowledge of nature as it is

"out there," knowledge obtained under controlled conditions in which fact and value and the knower and the known can be separated through use of fixed methods of inquiry. A central metaphysical presupposition is that all reality (not just the natural world) is inherently mathematical in nature and structure, human behavior not excluded, a belief that gave rise to the concept of "social science." Thus, our concern here is with the major paradigmatic shift from a mechanistically conceived epistemology that relies on a rationality of method, which abstracts and quantifies the human experience, to an interpretive and qualitative epistemology in which knowledge is seen to be constructed from our capacity to directly create and grasp meaning and connections in life. A finer-grained analysis of the concepts of positivism and interpretivism would render variations within these broad meanings but would, we believe, not alter these essential principles.

2. There are interpretations of postmodern deconstructionist thought that acknowledge sources of knowing outside of, or in reciprocity with, language (see, e.g., Kalamaras, 1994, a discussion of the generative function of silence in Blanchot's work).

2

Stories of Inner Change

How the loss of familiarity in everything had woken him up
and sharpened his senses!

Jill Paton Walsh (1995, p. 82)

A glance could lead to paragraphs of theory.

Michael Ondaatje (1992, p. 243)

Eureka!
Bathed in Transformation

James P. Anglin

It all began innocently enough, back in 1985. Over the course of several
years, I had been reviewing the literature on parent education and family
life education, searching for clues as to what I might do in order to help
parents to function more effectively as parents. I had been asked by a
local church minister to organize some sessions for parents, and had
done so making use of my own work background, parenting experience,
and reading in the work of such experts as Virginia Satir, the Gessell
Institute, and others. The sessions went well enough, at least on the level
of "expressed satisfaction" of participants, but I knew that there was a
lot more to learn about what parents really needed, and a lot more about
how I could better address these needs as an educator and facilitator.

My subsequent journey led me into further study of communication
skills, child development, normative family development, adult education, group process, and so on, finally leading to two areas that were
new to me, namely "social networks" and "social support." The traditional literature on parent and family life education had not yet discovered the powerful dimension of social support, and had not explored in
any systematic way the functioning and influence of informal and formal
networks. Thus emerged my proposal for a research project to analyze
the informal and formal helping networks of parents in Victoria, British
Columbia.

At this point, I should mention that earlier in my career, while doing
a Master of Social Work degree, I took a research course in which I had
to complete a series of weekly assignments that (mercifully) broke down
the required methodology and statistical learning into manageable (if
fragmented) bits. However, upon completing this course, I felt a certain
unease that I didn't really understand what research was all about. I
thought there must be more to this enterprise than I had grasped, and so

I approached the preeminent researcher on the faculty with my sensed deficit. He was most supportive, and provided me with a set of programmed learning materials that was to take me in more depth through the world of statistics. I took the materials home, and over a period of several weeks tried to learn what research was really all about. About halfway into the material, I gave up. I just couldn't get excited about what I was reading, and I returned the materials with a sense of personal and academic failure and inadequacy. Something must be wrong with me, I thought. I just couldn't get what this research "thing" was about. It all seemed so boring and trivial, and so divorced from any reality that was meaningful to me.

So, returning to my proposal to study parent networks, here I was, a budding academic with only this most unsatisfactory grounding in research, about to launch my first formal research project. I was searching for the appropriate method and place to begin.

In the course of my literature review, I had come across a Social Network Assessment (SNA) tool that had been used in a number of published studies reporting on the help-seeking patterns of parents (and others). My intention was to use this tool, with minor modifications, in a mail-out survey to a wide range of parents. I was pleased to be able to hire two very keen and bright students to work with me over a three-month period during the summer, and the project began.

After a number of meetings, a modified questionnaire instrument was developed containing several questions relating to the people and organizations that provided "help, support and encouragement" to the parent respondents. The format of these several latter questions consisted of a request for a listing of initials of each supportive person along with an indication of their relationship to the respondent (e.g., friend, spouse, co-worker, etc.). The specific instruction taken from the SNA instrument was: "Please list those people who are important to you at this time in your life. These are people with whom you have some contact (visit, talk to on the phone, do things with) at least once every 4–6 weeks."

When the draft was complete, I took it home for proofreading prior to sending it out for printing the next day. Arriving home, I decided to soak in a hot bath, and I brought the questionnaire with me into the bath to review. Perhaps as a result of the relaxing immersion in the soothing water and my letting go of the mental preoccupations of the day, it occurred to me to complete the questionnaire as if I were a respondent, rather than simply to proofread it. This proved to be a decisive moment in the project, and one of the most crucial decisions in my research career.

I began by writing "G.A.," the initials of my wife, and I wrote "spouse" in the space opposite. The next response was more difficult. I decided that "B.G." was number two on my list. I listed him as "friend." As I did so, I realized that although this was accurate, it could not possibly convey the nature of this relationship in my life to anyone reading this questionnaire. Recently, I had visited B.G. in Ottawa and we had shared a powerful experience in which we came to feel toward each other as brothers. It had been a profound and moving meeting for me especially, as (unlike B.G.) I had never had a biological brother, and I had never anticipated having such an experience in my life.

Significantly, this meeting had occurred six weeks and one day before completing the questionnaire, and I see or talk to B.G. only two or three times a year; therefore he would not even have qualified as a supporter under the SNA criterion! As I scribbled a note to this effect on the side of the questionnaire page, I could detect a sense of deep disquiet beginning to well up inside me. Someone who played a very significant role in my life, who I now carried in my heart, mind, and spirit on an ongoing basis, was being defined as "not important" because I didn't "visit, talk on the phone or do things with" him every four to six weeks. How presumptuous and misguided, I thought to myself.

The third on my list was "B.M." I hesitated a moment before I wrote those initials. Then I realized that I was avoiding writing "clergy." He was also a friend. Which relationship do I write? So I wrote "friend/ clergy." (How would the coder handle that one?) For number four on the list I put "A.P.," and this surprised me. Up to this moment I had not really thought of A.P. as one of my closest supporters, but he had actively supported me over a difficult year at work, and I realized that he had risen well up my "ladder" of supporters without me consciously realizing it.

At this point, I became strongly aware of the importance of systematically reflecting on one's relationships with others, and how provocative an exercise this (apparently) simple question-and-answer exercise turned out to be. I began to think of anonymous respondents sitting in the privacy of their own homes going through this exercise. What might be happening for them? What memories, regrets, insights, and emotional turmoil might be welling up in them? How would they be handling it?

As I proceeded to consider the fifth supporter, I became aware and surprised at the number of colleagues and relatives whom I was not putting on my list. I was especially disturbed at the realization that my father would not be on my list of supporters . . . anywhere! This realization saddened me greatly, as I was aware that for most of my prior life he would have been right near the top. What had happened? How had the emotional impact and the existential implications of this fact escaped me up to this moment? (A few days later, I had a powerful dream about my relationship with my father, and I described it to one of my research project students, who helped me to understand it more clearly. This experience led to a concerted effort on my part to heal the rift that had arisen so surreptitiously between my father and myself.)

By this point, my earlier sense of disquiet had become a strongly charged emotional reaction as I realized the degree to which sending out this "instrument" could constitute a significant intrusion into the psychic and emotional lives of the respondents. Why had no one mentioned this in the literature before? How had the university Research on Human Subjects Committee approved this instrument for use without cautioning me about this potential reaction? I began to feel a sense of betrayal, and a lack of trust in the validity of the studies I had been reading.

I was now in hot water (figuratively), and in cold water (literally), so I turned on the tap to heat up my bath; clearly I was going to be in here for a while yet! At one and the same time I was experiencing a strong sense of anxiety (almost panic) and an equally strong sense of exhilaration. Whatever was happening, and whatever the implications, I knew the experience would have a profound impact on my project, and likely on my research and academic career. I must have remained in the bathtub for forty-five minutes or more. I continued to write and to experience insight after insight, on a number of levels — questions arose in rapid succession about the design and impact of instrumentation, the meaning of reliability and validity, the ethics of research, the significance of supportive relationships, and so on. This was one of those rare moments when it was as if my brain had been opened up and some divine power was literally pouring knowledge into me. And it wasn't just into my mind, it was being poured into my body, my being, my very personhood. (As I write this, I am experiencing a rise in energy and excitement similar to the one I remember experiencing then. I pause . . .)

Dear reader, I have opened up my soul to you now, for an instant at least. I have made myself vulnerable publicly, as I was privately that day in the bathtub. I do not think it is necessary to further elaborate on the specifics of my particular insights of that day. I trust that you have a sufficient glimpse into this "transformational experience" to understand something of its significance in my development as a researcher.

But what came of this? (you might ask). The day after my own personal "Eureka" I arrived at my office with considerable anticipation. The visceral memories from the evening before were still etched in my mind and body. It was as if I were a biologist who had been gazing into his microscope the night before, and had discovered on the slide a new organism that he had never seen before. When the two students arrived, I asked each of them to take a copy of the draft questionnaire and to fill it out independently, as if they were actual respondents.

When they returned, I asked them what their experiences had been completing the forms. They began by describing the number of people they had identified, the various categories, and so on. I reframed the question: "What were your emotional and personal experiences when you began to formulate and write your responses? How much of your 'social support' reality is reflected in your actual responses? Were you surprised by any of your responses?"

They responded readily to this permission to express their private thoughts and feelings, and some of their reactions echoed some of mine from the night before. An animated discussion among the three of us ensued, which spread well beyond our immediate responses to this particular questionnaire. One of the students described feelings related to previous work as a research assistant on another project implementing the "Home Inventory" checklists. The experience had been very negative, leaving behind feelings of being a spy, devious and unethical. The role of observer, recording and coding the home life "reality" of families, utilizing a reductionistic instrument, had brought home how inadequate, distorting, and demeaning this (supposedly) objective approach had been, not only for the "reality" of the family being "measured," but also for the reality of the research assistants who were hired and trained to complete this task. They were hired to follow instructions, and to apply the instrument strictly according to the criteria provided, and there had been no permission or opportunity to discuss or debrief this experience. As a result, this student was still carrying considerable resentment and some guilt and embarrassment at having been part of such a questionable process. There was genuine relief at finally being able to voice feelings and to assess the experience, and to explore implications for the student personally and academically, and as a beginning researcher.

I recall my own feelings of vulnerability in sharing my bathtub experiences with the students, and in admitting to them that I felt the need to trust them with my doubts, fears, and questions. We honestly wondered if we could proceed with the study that I had been funded, and they had been hired, to do. All three of us had concerns about the validity and reliability of any questionnaire instrument we could devise, and also about the ethical implications of intervening in parents' lives in this manner. Our discussion was characterized by openness and self-disclosure; we experienced a new depth in our relationships with each other, and a more profound understanding of the process in which we were engaged.

In the end, we concluded that we could only approach parents who were already in a support group. We would have them complete a questionnaire as a prelude to an open dialogue about how they responded, and what the meanings of their responses were for the reality of their supporters and support networks, their characteristics, and what these meant to them as parents.

But I was still quite nervous about this new direction, and I was not aware of any precedent for this approach. Was it really valid and rigorous enough? What would my colleagues think about it? As I was searching about for a new sense of stability and a foundation for our work, I came across a copy of *Naturalistic Inquiry* by Yvonna Lincoln and Egon Guba (1985). The experience of reading this book brought considerable relief and a sense of validation. I was not crazy or incompetent. Even one of the most noted gurus of evaluation and statistics, Egon Guba, was now questioning the traditional foundations of much traditional social science research! Even though I have come to see limitations in this text, it will always hold a treasured place in my research library.

However, even though a new research plan had emerged, we were not out of the woods yet! Given the significant shifts that were taking place in the project, I was concerned with how the Dean of Research Administration might react to the new manner in which I intended to spend the research grant that had been obtained on the basis of a very different proposal.

I submitted the revised materials for review by the Research on Human Subjects Committee, and waited. A few days later, I received a curt message that the Dean wished to meet with me as soon as possible. I thought to myself that this would surely constitute a major black mark on my (young) research record. I remember walking across the campus heading for the Dean's office, feeling like a convict going to hear his sentencing by the judge. My two project colleagues wished me luck and waited anxiously to learn the fate of their summer employment.

The Dean was a well-respected researcher, a psychologist who was well versed in traditional research and statistical methods; in brief, she had a reputation for being "hard-nosed." I entered her office prepared for the worst, and I was surprised by the friendliness of her greeting. She proceeded to apologize for the hasty message that she had left, but she knew I was ready to go ahead with my project and she did not want to hold me up. She suggested two or three small wording changes to the letters and background information materials for parents, and I readily accepted them all. When she concluded her comments, I could not resist asking her if she had noticed that the study was taking a somewhat different direction from my original proposal. She replied that she had noticed that, and that she supported the shift. She acknowledged that there were essentially two ways of going about this kind of research; one was to have preconceived categories and frameworks with which to capture the data, and the other (mine) was to go in as open-mindedly as possible in order to learn from the respondents themselves before attempting to categorize or codify the phenomena under study.

I do not know to what degree I showed my relief and ecstatic inner reaction, but I felt deeply grateful to this person for her understanding. I returned to the waiting students and poured out the story of the meeting. Reinforced by this support from the Dean, and bolstered by the precedent of *Naturalistic Inquiry*, we felt free to shape a new (at least to us) paradigm approach to understanding parents' social networks and social support.

On the basis of our recent experiences, we had come to realize, affectively as well as intellectually, that questionnaire responses are often (always?) meager and misleading indications of what respondents actually think and feel, and that an apparently simple and straightforward question can be deeply intrusive and may elicit powerful and disturbing reactions (immediate and longer term) from the respondents. We also came to understand that we have a moral responsibility to be aware of the potential impact of such seemingly innocuous questions (intrusions), and an ethical responsibility to help the respondents to deal with the impact, even if it is unpredictable and unanticipated. Perhaps most importantly, it was clear to us that the distinction between research and intervention is not tenable, and that research involving persons is a significant form of intervention into their lives.

Since the completion of the parent networks study, I have been fortunate to spend a study leave reading widely in the qualitative, interpretive, and "new paradigm" research literature, searching for more dialogical and participatory forms of human inquiry. I have been gratified to discover many researchers who have been willing to share the stories of their struggles toward methods and strategies that more adequately disclose the ambiguous, fragile, and often-hidden realities of human experience. It appears to me that we may have entered a significant period of transition in human science research characterized by a profound re-appreciation of what it means to be human, and, therefore, what it means to be human beings trying to understand ourselves and our fellow human beings.

Paradigm Lost and Regained

KEITH BALLARD

In my journeys through different research interests and paradigm loyalties, there have been some particular moments of delight, amazement, or despair that signaled that it was time to confront something basic about my work and my place in it. The initial experience was predominantly emotional, and it was not always clear exactly what was involved. Eventually I sorted out what I thought were the key issues and wrote an intellectual justification for each new focus or direction, but the origin of the changes went far deeper than these accounts showed. To the extent that I can reconstruct past experiences, here is what I never wrote of at the time, what I often failed to acknowledge as an essential part of what was happening, but what finding and losing paradigms actually felt like.

An early but still easily recalled experience was one of having to repress much of what I understood life to be about. At the time it seemed to be a necessary component of research training that I, and things important to me, were set aside so that a supposedly "objective" and therefore "scientific" understanding of the world could be achieved. Generations of students, my own included, have been persuaded to such a view. No doubt many still are. But when, almost 20 years later, I moved from positivist to interpretivist thought, it felt like coming home. I remember a sense of relief, a sense of harmony restored between how I learned about the world personally in my everyday life and how I thought about the world through research.

My introduction to a scientific worldview was through my training as a teacher, and later as a psychologist and researcher. It seemed evident that ordinary people, with beliefs, doubts, and passions, had no place in educational or psychological research. There were subjects, who were useful for generating data, and researchers, who were impersonal recorders and manipulators of variables independent of themselves. I accepted this, despite having some exposure to investigations that did describe people and the complexity of their lives, and to researchers who wrote about themselves and their work. For example, in studying sociology at the undergraduate level, I had thrilled to W. F. Whyte's (1955) *Street Corner Society* and his account of doing the research, with all of its personal involvement and uncertainties. I had identified with Jackson and Marsden's (1962) *Education and the Working Class*, which included accounts of working-class students in an English grammar school. That is where I had come from, and I understood the experiences of the students while admiring the researchers' admission that the story was also about themselves.

Nevertheless, I turned away from such studies toward a quantitative approach for my own work. Perhaps I thought that science was not something you were supposed to identify with and enjoy. I remember a sense of regret that "real" science could not include the interesting people that I had met in some of these sociological studies. Whatever the case, circumstances and I together contrived toward a belief in "hard" data and the distant, objective scientist. My own study of high school students and their aspirations was a mathematical tale of regression coefficients and factor analysis in which neither the students nor I appeared.

And then came the rats. I well recall the day I was introduced to Skinner and animal training. My reaction was one of disbelief and a sense of anger. I could not see how anyone could equate animal conditioning with human experience, with the world of John Donne and Doris Lessing, Thomas Hardy and Anita Desai. Yet, some years later, I began a long commitment to applied behavior analysis. Once again I set off along a path leading away from my personal ways of knowing. I was even aware of a chasm, a seismic fault, with which we are familiar in New Zealand, separating my sense of me as a person from my sense of myself as a psychologist and researcher. So for a considerable time I lived in two worlds, experiencing in one a passion for objectivity, prediction, and control, and in the other the joy of enchantment, uncertainty, and liberation.

After a few years in elementary teaching I undertook further training to work as a child psychologist. In this role I was attracted to applied behavior analysis by its precision, its explanatory elegance, and its explicit purpose of using a scientific method to solve human problems. I had always opposed the meaningless rituals of psychological testing, the medical-model writing of jargon-ridden stories taken from normative comparisons with averaged others. Applied behavior analysis was a viable, interactive alternative, and among educators in New Zealand it had a humanistic face. We rejected packaged behavioral technology such as precision teaching and the simplistic task analysis and token approaches of animal behaviorism, emphasizing instead the analysis of more naturalistic approaches to instruction. This did, of course, mean a focus on quantitative data, but also it meant collaborating with parents and teachers in joint problem-solving in their homes and schools.

In 1976 I was teaching and researching in applied behavior analysis at the University of Otago in New Zealand. As part of a postgraduate course that I taught, I arranged student practicums so that my students could gain experience in behavioral instruction. Mostly this involved work with adults who had an intellectual disability. The clients, usually with input from their support agency, would say what they wanted to learn. Students would then be available across three months to help them with money skills, shopping, telling the time, recreational games, work tasks, using the telephone, social skills, doing the laundry, operating a cassette recorder, using the bus system, budgeting, banking, and more.

This work was undertaken using a research format, but as we wrote the journal accounts of behaviors observed and changed, I knew that there was always something missing. In particular, there was no record of the delight in this work that came from people supporting one another as they learned together, nor was there evidence of the informal student learning that occurred around disability issues. Eventually I wrote about the value of what I described as these "additional" student and client outcomes, but I experienced increasing discomfort about what I said we were doing — demonstrating effective behavioral instruction — and what I sensed was the really important part of our teaching — the quality of the relationship between the teacher and the learner, unmediated by the behavioral strategies.

In other research I identified multiple collateral outcomes from behavioral interventions with children who had intellectual disabilities, and wrote about interpersonal factors, including affect, in accounts of behavioral teaching interactions. The more complicated the models became, the less satisfying the explanations appeared. It was like painting with numbers. In the end there was a picture there, but it lacked depth, meaning, soul. I introduced qualitative data into research reports and began to work with ecological models. I was attempting to integrate Bronfenbrenner's (1979) phenomenological perspective, which emphasizes the environment as it is perceived by the developing person, with what I thought of as objective data. Then one of those vivid moments occurred that told me the nature of the problem I was dealing with.

Along with a postgraduate student, I was teaching a man to write his name. It proved a challenging task for him and for us, but over several months he eventually reached his goal of independently signing for his own paycheck, for his savings bank account, and so on. Some weeks later, agency staff told me that as a result of this new learning the man had gained in self-confidence, "stood taller," and was more outgoing. It would be good, I thought, if these things could be true, but in the absence of clearer definitions of the behaviors and firm evidence for causal effects, it seemed that there were no grounds for believing in them. Then I went to see him in order to say thanks for working with the student, and saw immediately that he was not the somewhat retiring person we had known initially. Why had I not believed what the staff, whom I respected and trusted, had told me? Of course, I could think of many competing hypotheses regarding the origins of the changes that the staff had reported, but the fact was that they knew the person and were confident in identifying the writing skill as a source of a new sense of self.

It was disorienting to realize that my research perspective was doing more than eliciting a sensible, scientific caution in my work. It was, I felt, shutting me off from ordinary human judgment, experiences, emotions, and common sense that I wanted to be part of.

There was a wider context for this incident. At the time, I was beginning to work with some Maori people on disability and related issues. I began to learn about the holistic perspective of this culture that does not separate the person from their land or from their spiritual and tribal worlds. This made me even more acutely aware of the inconsistencies between my research and my personal ways of knowing, the latter seeming to mesh comfortably with what I understood of a Maori worldview. I was also working in the school system on integration of the disabled through mainstreaming, with increasing involvement at the administrative and policy level rather than at the level of the individual child. From this came the final push toward paradigm change.

Across several years I wrote about mainstreaming, telling the stories of children with disabilities, their parents, and their teachers as they struggled for resources and for inclusion over exclusion. This attracted criticism from some researchers and administrators who claimed that in supporting mainstreaming I was not attending to data, was biased, emotional, and politically motivated. One day it struck me how, in their sense, that was all true. They thought that there could be an objective position, untainted by people's passions and commitments. What I was suggesting, along with others in the integration movement, was that the right of the disabled to be included in regular classroom settings was not simply an issue of research data. It was, and is, fundamentally an issue of values, of how we choose to conceptualize others and our relationships with them. It was true that these ideological issues were not separate from my research program—they had *become* my research program. It was now time to acknowledge this, and to evaluate its implications for my work in the social sciences and in professional practice.

I can remember the room I was in on this particular day in 1988. In fact, for each of the moments I refer to in this account, I can recall the setting and circumstances with great clarity. A meeting with some education administrators had ended, yet again, with expression of their concern about "bias" in research on mainstreaming, and about "emotional" advocacy for integration. In the past, such criticism had always worried me, as it should. Critical self-reflection requires that we rigorously challenge our motivations, ideas, and assumptions from alternative perspectives. But it does not require the pretense that we believe in nothing, that our work is independent of our values. It was this realization that struck me with physical force that day. There was the problem. I had been trying to live in two incompatible worlds. I was clinging to my training in the idea that science was detached and value-free, and so became anxious when challenged from that position. Yet I knew that I was learning far more from involvement with people and with issues I was committed to than I ever had as a distant recorder of events that happened to others. It was time to end that tension. As I walked out of the meeting, I knew that the sense of division, that chasm between what I believed in and how I thought about research, was over. Something that had felt wrong for a long time now felt resolved; the seismic plates had shifted and settled, for a while, at least. I was thinking of Doris Lessing and Toni Morrison, whose recent work was still surging through me, and I knew that now I had to try to make these ways of understanding as relevant to my research life as they had always been to my more general struggle to make sense of the world and our place in it. When the earth really does move, it resolves stress that has built up over a long time. Both above and below the surface, things are changed.

That moment confirmed for me that I need no longer work from a positivist worldview. I would no longer break the world down into discrete bits for study, nor pretend that I could separate who I am from what I do. As a result, I have continued to seek involvement with others as a participant learner, open to a range of interpretations, constructions, and reconstructions, and confronting problems of ideology, power, and purpose in research and researchers.

I do not claim that positivism has been my false consciousness, absorbed through prevailing climates in teaching, child psychology, or research. That would imply too passive a role on my part. The decision made to use multivariate statistics, to revel in the flexible elegance of repeated measures and single-subject designs, and to attempt to combine qualitative and behavioral data satisfied my need for secure knowledge through proper techniques, and for a research model that was pleasing in both an aesthetic sense and in terms of apparent explanatory power. There was also, I am sure, the need for expertise, for the power this accrues, and for recognition from professional peers.

My current work also meets personal needs, but these no longer include certainty in research method and outcome. Having experienced research as alienation, as estrangement from the people I set out to understand, my present need is for the uncertainty and complexity of ordinary interpersonal relationships. So, I have joined with parents, teachers, and others to write stories of inclusive education and to try to achieve the participatory and emancipatory goals of action research. Our understandings are emerging from shared ideas focused on problems of policy and practice. There are no simple issues. Both the problems and their solutions exist in the ways we imagine that the world is and could be. We construct our understandings through dialogue with one another and with the many poets and other storytellers that we choose to illuminate our lives.

On Becoming

CURT DUDLEY-MARLING

The telling of my story begins in 1981 with my dissertation, in which I investigated the ability of students labeled "learning disabled" (LD) to use language effectively in social settings. This topic was encouraged by studies that concluded that difficulties with the social use of language contributed to the relatively low social status of students with learning disabilities. I designed an experiment to assess the pragmatic skills of LD and non-LD students, focusing on students' ability to adjust the politeness of their requests according to listener characteristics such as age and status. I used the Wide Range Achievement Test to ensure "significant" differences in academic ability between LD and non-LD subjects. And, because I was concerned that the small sample sizes would not produce "normal" distributions, I used non-parametric statistics to analyze the data.

Even before I completed my study, I recognized a serious contradiction in the methodology. Pragmatics is "the ability to use language in context," but my study would indicate only how LD students used language in the situation I had contrived. My study said nothing about how they used language in the range of social settings they encountered naturally in their lives in and out of school. I was so concerned with designing a "good" experiment that I ignored what I knew about language! But I felt I had to get on with my life, so I finished my dissertation and kept my doubts to myself.

Nevertheless, it wasn't long before I rejected the basic assumption on which my dissertation was based: that students with learning disabilities have relatively low social status. The more I thought about it, it didn't make sense that ALL students with learning disabilities were unpopular. The problem seemed to be the experimental method itself, which obscured individual differences among students who were labeled learning disabled. The few studies that presented more detailed data revealed that some students with learning disabilities were unpopular,

From Positivism to Interpretivism and Beyond: Tales of Transformation in Educational and Social Research (The Mind-Body Connection). Copyright © 1996 by Teachers College, Columbia University. All rights reserved. ISBN 0-8077-3534-5. Prior to photocopying items for classroom use, please contact the Copyright Clearance Center, Customer Service, 222 Rosewood Dr., Danvers, MA 01923, USA, tel. (508) 750-8400.

but many were well liked. And, of course, it is not uncommon for non-LD persons to be disliked!

This recognition led me to suspect all experimental research based on the mythical "average" child, and I began to doubt the concept of learning disabilities itself. The utility of the concept of learning disabilities depends on the assumption that there exists a group of students (i.e., students with learning disabilities) who share a set of instructionally relevant characteristics. Yet it seemed to me that while these characteristics may describe a statistically constructed average LD child, they do not describe individual LD students.

It seems that my dissertation was a major turning point for me, a transforming experience. Perhaps it was, but it was not an isolated beginning. I had long been uncomfortable with my behaviorist roots. Early in my teaching career I had no difficulty filling up my teaching days with perceptual, fine-, and gross-motor activities, but I was never satisfied that my LD students were learning anything worthwhile. My students had no enthusiasm for balance beams and language drills, and neither did I. We were all bored. Our recesses kept getting longer. And I felt inadequate.

But this begs the question: What was there about me that made me so uncomfortable with behaviorism? Many of my teaching colleagues, all of whom were intelligent, dedicated professionals, embraced behaviorism without reservations. Why did I resist and search for other options? I recently heard a talk by Fred Erickson (1994) that has led me to consider the role my personal biography has played in my discomfort with definitive accounts of human behavior. I recall that as a child I was uncomfortable with the certain truths that were so much a part of my Catholic schooling. Perhaps I was naturally disinclined to accept absolutist explanations; more likely, however, I resented the power vested in those who possessed canonical knowledge. I have long suspected the relationship between my religious upbringing and my resentment of authority, but writing this has been the first time that I have considered the possibility that rejecting my Catholic background may have been a factor in my discomfort with the deterministic worldview.

Early in my teaching career I took a language development course from Richard Kretschmer at the University of Cincinnati that provided a theoretical basis for me to begin challenging the behavioral assumptions underpinning my teaching, but, although I wasn't aware of it at the time, my teaching continued to be plagued by ambiguities, contradictions, and uncertainties. For example, I learned from Richard how complex language and language learning are, but in my work with children, I continued to rely on standardized tests that were informed by a particularly narrow view of language. I finally abandoned standardized tests in favor of informal observation, but my assessment practices continued to show strong quantitative influences. When I was a learning disability teacher in Green Bay, Wisconsin, my assessment reports featured statements such as "45% of her oral reading miscues change the meaning of the text" or "30% of reading miscues are grammatically unacceptable," without any consideration of how factors such as purpose, background knowledge, and the text itself affected how students went about making sense of texts. But, of course, "30% of miscues are grammatically unacceptable" applied only to the text on which the students were evaluated. For example, one of my students produced a significant number of miscues with some texts, but produced almost none when he read books with which he was more familiar.

When I finally began my doctoral studies, statistics and experimental research courses were a major focus of my program even though, by that time, I had rejected standardized tests, concluding that they were "acontextual." This didn't strike me as inconsistent. I was interested in alternative assessment procedures, but it didn't occur to me to search for alternative research methods. I'm not even sure I was aware that there were alternative research methods. I had read Ruth Benedict and Margaret Mead and I was familiar with Piaget's work, and much of the language development literature that had such a profound effect on my thinking was based on case studies. I knew the results of this research, but I had given little explicit thought to the method.

An invitation from Lynn Rhodes when I was at the University of Colorado–Denver to do an ethnography with her may have been what started me on the process of reflecting on the why of method. I accepted her invitation without letting on that I didn't have the slightest idea what ethnography was. We did our study, but it would be several years before I would fully appreciate qualitative research as a method. In the meantime, the contradictions persisted. Two years after Lynn and I did our classroom ethnography — perhaps influenced by the traditional research culture at the University of Colorado — we started an experimental study of the reading comprehension of learning-disabled and non–learning-disabled students in which we asked students to read a piece of nonfiction and then retell what they had read.

We spent several months collecting and analyzing our data, but we couldn't make sense of it. Were we measuring reading comprehension? Students' reading of our intentions? Students' verbal skills? I learned the lessons of my dissertation all over again: When students read, write, or talk in contrived settings, you only learn about students' reading, writing, and talking in contrived settings.

My move from a behavioral to a holistic framework has been gradual. There isn't a defining moment or crucial insight. There are no "aha's" in my story. But my story isn't over. A close examination of my work would, I am certain, reveal lingering contradictions, and my thinking continues to grow. Two years ago I took a leave from the university to teach 3rd grade. Nothing I have done in my professional life has pushed my thinking further or faster. Making sense of 3rd grade has increased my ability to live with uncertainty and has strengthened my "writer's voice." Confronting issues of gender, race, and ethnicity on a daily basis as a classroom teacher has also had the effect of politicizing my work. These three themes — learning to live with uncertainty, strengthening my writer's voice, and politicizing my work — are important in my personal and professional development and are, I think, worthy of further exploration.

Living with Uncertainty

A basic tenet of holism is that the world is a complex place. That's what makes determinism so unsatisfying for me — it fails to account for the complexity of our lives and the world in which we live. But acknowledging the infinite complexity of the universe makes certainty problematic, and that can be unsettling. I have long been conscious of my own uncertainty, but it has been a private concern. I rarely acknowledged my uncertainty publicly because, I suspect, I was concerned with threats to my credibility. Students and journal editors expect certainty. At least, that's what I believed.

I think that it was my increasing discomfort with uncertainty that led me to return to the classroom, to embark on a personal "quest for certainty" (Dewey, 1960). What I knew about language and literacy development, for example, had increased over the years, but I was sure of less, and my confidence waned. What I needed, I reasoned, was to renew my practice, and teaching 3rd grade would make me more certain. But it didn't work out that way. Teaching Denise, for example, was complicated by suspicions of abuse. Reading instruction for Razika, Roya, and Shyrose was confounded by issues of language and culture. My transactional view of literacy conflicted with Ali's religious belief that some texts are to be read literally. I sometimes worried that pushing Fatima, Nader, and Benizar to write on more personal topics may have clashed with their cultural values. Schools and classrooms are very complicated places. The pretense of certainty, such as that implied in lockstep curricula, ignores this fact.

Uncertainty has emerged as a dominant theme in my analysis of my teaching experience. I have been influenced by the work of Deborah Britzman (1991) and Joseph McDonald (1992) to accept uncertainty as a natural part of teaching and of the human experience, and to value it as a source of reflection and growth.

Strengthening My Voice

Early in my career I adopted the conventional style of writing in the third person. This style, I was assured, would help protect me from my subjective self. But I am not a neutral thing, "the writer," "the researcher," or "the author." I am Curt Dudley-Marling—teacher, author, son, husband, father. A particular writing style—or method—does not protect me or anyone else from personal, "subjective" influences. The questions I ask and how I understand and interpret data are affected by my distinct experiences and background knowledge. Hiding the "I" is a pretense, a fraud that forces me to hide my passion, to deny who I am, and to pretend that my words are separate from me. Acknowledging the "I" allows me to reveal myself and my feelings. It also reminds me and my readers that my data, or whatever I present, have been filtered through the temporal lens of that distinctive being called Curt Dudley-Marling, a white middle-class male who has been shaped by his culture, class, race, and personal experiences. Writing about my experience as a 3rd grade teacher has heightened my awareness of who "I" is and how an ever-changing "I" affects my understanding and interpretation of my own experiences. Making this explicit does a service to me and my readers.

Making My Work Political

An evolving understanding of the complexity of context led me to reject the results of my dissertation. Context has been a major theme in my work ever since. But my understanding of context continues to become more complex. Language and literacy, for example, cannot be understood apart from purpose, audience, and the social and political relations of speakers and listeners and readers and writers. Analyzing, interpreting, and theorizing about my experience as a 3rd grade teacher has pushed me to recognize the importance of the broader political context of schools and society. I cannot make sense of Charles as a reader, for example, without confronting the fact that he is a black male who lives in public housing. Nor could I understand Razika's and Benizar's reluctance to participate in gender-mixed literature sharing groups without taking up the issues of gender and culture.

I understand better now the importance of considering race, class, and gender when trying to make sense of what goes on in classrooms. Language and literacy are still important to me, but I no longer see them as the ultimate goal of schooling. There is much more to schooling than "reading, writing, and 'rithmetic." Language and literacy are important only insofar as they help people examine and, it is hoped, improve the conditions of their lives and help us and our students create a more just and equitable world to live in.

On Becoming an Interpretist: From Knowing as a Teacher to Knowing as a Researcher

Deborah J. Gallagher

My journey toward becoming an interpretist, like that of others, no doubt has very personal roots. In tracing the nature of this journey, I know I have made both conscious and subconscious choices about what is important in life. My years as a teacher in the public schools likely had considerable influence, so I will begin there. In my teacher "training" programs, I learned to think and act reductively. I became skilled in developing and delivering highly organized, linear lessons, which, from all accounts, were the mark of a competent teacher. My teaching plans always included behavioral objectives and step-by-step procedures that I would follow to reach *my* goals *for them*. These objectives were derived from wonderful scope and sequence charts, and each skill was task-analyzed. I designed highly specific evaluation procedures that would indicate unequivocally whether the students were learning these skills. It made eminent good sense to me at the time that if I carefully used these prescriptive methods, success would surely follow. Method was everything. The more control I exercised, the better. But that is not how it turned out.

For the most part, teaching was a drill, one that I endured because that is what I thought was required of me professionally. My students were not similarly inclined to pick up the cross, though. Sure, for the most part, they were compliant. They marched through the assignments, listened dutifully, and participated. Yet skills that they had "learned" soon became "forgotten," and life in the classroom seemed not a little void of meaning. My initial response to this was to step up my efforts. I become exhausted just thinking about it now. At that point, though, I figured more was better. I had not begun to suppose that teaching and learning could not be mechanized. It had not occurred to me that adherence to a reductive mindset kept me from seeing and prevented me from responding to the complex human environment of the classroom. In fact, I was oblivious to the idea that I possessed any particular mindset at all. I implicitly believed that the way I viewed teaching and learning was not a matter of choice, it was simply "the way it was."

So, I believed that my goals were preeminent in their legitimacy because I "knew" what was best for my students. Life was simple, then, but frustrating. It seemed that despite their seeming compliance, many of my students had other ideas. Only after a number of years (I was a slow learner) did I begin to see glimmers of the possibility that this reductive approach was flawed and was not necessarily helping my students, or me for that matter. This reversal represented a real departure from my professional preparation.

To give the reader an example that is representative of those which pushed me along in my journey, I'll take you back several years ago to a bright, cold winter day in a classroom where I taught eleven- and twelve-year-old students with learning disabilities.

On that afternoon, I was conducting a social studies lesson on map-reading skills. As I drew a crude illustration (I am no artist) of the globe with lines of latitude and longitude on the board, one of my students, Shane, loudly announced that the illustration was wrong. "The lines aren't even," he declared angrily. And he was right. Then he added with finality, "You don't know what you're talking about." Stunned by the outburst and not a little threatened by his accusation, I defended myself by explaining that I was only trying to describe the general concept of latitude and longitude and that the lines did not have to be precise in order for them to understand this. But Shane would not let go. He slammed his textbook closed and glared angrily out of the window overlooking the asphalt-covered playground outside. I attempted to regroup my sensibilities. Noting that Shane's outburst met with the approval of the other eight students, I directed their attention to the text's illustration of the globe and went on with my explanation, which got me, gratefully, through the remainder of the social studies period.

My first instinct was to be very angry with Shane for his rudeness. My greatest fear was that his anger would spread, and that soon I would have some sort of insurrection on my hands. Naturally, as a good behavior manager, I began to plan for "managing" future disruptions on his part.

At some point during that long afternoon and evening as my mind replayed the incident, I began to wonder what had inspired the explosion. It finally occurred to me that Shane was looking to challenge my authority and to exert a sense of power in the classroom. And for some unknown reason, I was able to consider the possibility that he and the other students were trying to tell me that life in my classroom left them feeling incompetent and powerless. Perhaps he was trying to get me to understand that he and the other students had trouble learning in traditional ways, something I already "knew" in some sort of factual way, but did not understand in any real way because I continued, for the most part, to practice these traditional methods. The only means he had for telling me this was by attempting to discredit me. It made sense. After all, wasn't I discrediting him on a daily basis by compelling him to learn my way? If someone had to be wrong here, and clearly someone had a problem, why not the teacher? Why not, indeed?

Over time, helped along by my students' needs to keep their integrity intact, and to save myself from emptiness, I began to move away from traditional methods. I suppose I sensed the importance of understanding and being in tune with them, rather than trying to control them. Forcing our world into a neat package just wasn't working. Gradually I noticed that I was changing the way I worked and interacted with them. I began to pay more attention to the things they talked about and the topics that interested them. These interests found their way into my teaching. Instead of having them complete exercises in their grammar text, we spent more time writing stories, essays, and letters with a purpose in mind. For example, we wrote stories, sequels to stories we had read together, and letters to real people. They learned the conventions of writing as they began to understand the purpose of these rules in making themselves clear to their audience. I read to them more frequently, and made time to listen to them talk about the things they read, both in school and out.

The way I "managed" behavior changed, too. I found myself asking questions instead of passing edicts or dishing out rewards and penalties. Often I learned that my students had some very sane reasons for acting as they did. Sometimes they did not know what motivated them to act in certain ways, but in talking about it, they began to gain insight. At other times, we never got to the bottom of it, but my attempts to understand seemed to have a calming, comforting effect. I learned quite a bit, and so did they.

As I said, this change did not happen overnight. In fact, I was only tacitly aware that a change was occurring at all. To work with my students in this way required me to relinquish the precision and control I was used to having. Ironically, I began to sense that it was no great loss; instead, I was laying down a tremendously heavy burden. My students, I felt, began to like school better also. The feeling of constant struggle began to subside, and so did the emptiness.

This, I think, was when I first began to grapple with the costs of holding a reductionist view of the world in my work. At the time, I didn't know it per se. I only knew that what I was doing did not match what I wanted to accomplish. Yet my teaching experiences represented a first step in the direction of questioning both the legacy and legitimacy of this perspective.

While I was completing my doctoral studies, it began to dawn on me that positivistic research methods constituted more of the same way of knowing, thinking, and acting that I had already rejected. As I took semester after semester of quantitative research methods, I found it very hard to take seriously the notion that we could predict (much less control) human behavior by accounting for all of the variables that ostensibly influence people. And even if we could do so in an experimental setting, as it was thought could be done, what would that mean for the complexity of real life? I was, of course, pondering the external validity question as discussed by Cook and Campbell (1979), except for me it was not enough to acknowledge it as a problem. Further, I was nagged by how little bearing all of this emphasis on quantification had on my previous nine years in the classroom. For me these questions rendered quantitative research methods more than just meaningless. Had they been only meaningless, it would have been merely a waste of time. I began to see, however, that the same need for the external, unauthentic power I had tried to force on my students in my early years of teaching likewise shaped the need for quantitative, statistical models of inquiry. The superimposition of these modes and methods on educational phenomena is no more, and no less, than insisting it is our privilege to have control over others and over life. It has little to do with knowledge. Certainly numbers are clean and orderly, as were my reductionistic teaching methods. One can impose order without permission, and that feels powerful; but I had already learned to mistrust that kind of power. I had tasted the fruit of it. These and other issues floated around in my mind early in my doctoral program, but I never expressed them for fear of appearing as if I were somehow missing the point.

I also felt that there was an exclusivity about all of this that implied a hierarchy. The classroom teacher was on the bottom of the hierarchy, the university researcher was at the top. This seemed inappropriate and unjust. The more I understood about quantitative research methodology, the less impressed I became.

In the fall semester of my second year, I enrolled in a course on qualitative research with little background except that I understood case studies and qualitative research to be related in some way. It was at this point that everything changed. When I read scholars who challenged the tenets of the positivistic perspective, I felt both relieved and vindicated, very much the way I felt when I relinquished reductionistic methods of teaching. I also felt deeply disturbed by two things. First, I was angry with myself for not trusting my instincts. Why was I so afraid to challenge what I had learned to this point? It was as if I had almost been married off to a strange man, and I hadn't raised a single protest. I was amazed and embarrassed that I had exercised so little skepticism.

Second, I wondered why faculty who embraced positivistic research methods seemed unperturbed by the challenges the interpretive paradigm posed, if they had been aware of them. How could they continue to espouse quantitative research methods in light of these conflicts? In fairness, I think those who embrace the positivistic perspective are well intentioned, as I was as a teacher who employed reductionistic teaching methods. I had the interests of my students at heart. I believe that positivistic researchers are equally dedicated to advancing knowledge in their field.

Too, it is difficult to let go of the ways we have been taught to understand the world. I don't think I would have been open to change if I had not been so entirely dissatisfied with the results of reductive ways of teaching and knowing. For me to gain another perspective, I had to get outside of myself for a period of time. The sum total of lived experiences and the intellectual influences of scholars (those whom I know personally and those whom I know through their published work) provided the catalyst for growth and change. I am grateful for the contributions of those who helped me along the way. It has been an inevitable journey in that, retrospectively, I can hardly imagine having chosen another road. There are many questions still to consider. I don't expect conclusive answers. Having become an interpretist, I understand too well that questions and answers will be continually rethought, refelt, and reconstructed.

What Happened to Me on the Road to Damascus

Egon G. Guba

I began life as a positivist and somehow got transmogrified into what I choose to call a constructivist. How did it happen? Was it a sudden conversion along the road to Damascus? Or was it something more uncertain and indecisive, more tacit than explicit, a steady accretion more evolutionary than revolutionary?

I received more than the usual exposure to positivism in my formative student years. I did undergraduate majors and even some graduate work in physics and mathematics before switching to statistics and measurement, in which I completed both master's and doctoral degrees. Shortly thereafter I was teaching in these fields and carrying out good positivist research (most notably, testing the so-called Getzels-Guba model of administrative staff relations). I never questioned the wisdom of what I was doing.

By 1961 I had been appointed Director of the Bureau of Educational Research and Service at the Ohio State University. It was then, as a putative "expert" in administration in my first administrative position, that I began experiencing the nagging feeling that my positivist faith may have been misplaced. I had a brief honeymoon as director, but then a two-hour-long altercation with one of the Bureau staff, very much senior to me in age and experience, shattered my illusions (I lost the argument!). When I finally got him out of my office, I fell back into my overstuffed administrator's chair and said to myself, "Okay, wiseguy, you're supposed to be one of the world's experts on administrative staff relations; why is it that you let that man trample all over you?" The theory that Getzels and I had devised was supposed to help administrators deal with such staffing problems, but it had obviously not helped me! I began to suspect that scientific generalizations might not be just the right thing to draw on in solving practical problems, that there existed a major gap between theory and practice. My belly felt strangely disquieted.

Nevertheless, I persevered in the old ways. Several Bureau colleagues and I undertook a classic positivist study of eye movements of children watching television (it failed, but we wrote that off as a technical problem in data analysis). I helped Daniel Stufflebeam devise the Context-Input-Process-Product model of evaluation, itself a rational/technical approach that was advertised as useful in "servicing decision-makers." So I survived that winter of my discontent, continuing on the positivist road despite the unease in my gut.

But then came Project Discovery. During my third year as director, two men appeared in my office, one a special consultant to the Bell & Howell Corporation, the other the president of Encyclopedia Britannica Films. What they wanted was a Bureau evaluation of a demonstration project in which four schools, widely separated geographically, would be provided with a very large number of films and filmstrips and all the associated hardware. The decisions about how to use them would, however, be left entirely in the hands of the teachers and administrators involved. My response was quick (they did, after all, have check in hand). I would be delighted; I knew just how to do that; all I needed to start was a list of objectives. No, no, they responded, we don't have any objectives, we just want to know what will happen. The evaluators were simply to be "flies on the wall," letting whatever happened happen, and being careful themselves not to serve as channels of communication from one person to another about new and interesting applications.

No one in my memory had ever talked about an evaluation that way; would it really be possible? I recruited four graduate students, each of whom would live at one of the sites. During the first summer we met all day every day, deciding what information we would collect and how we would collect it. In retrospect, I realize that we reinvented many wheels that were already well developed by ethnographers, but that were new to us.

The project ran for two years, and left me stunned with the insights we were able to gain by simple observation and interview techniques. And there was hardly a variable or a correlation or a measurement instrument in sight. But when I delivered a paper focusing on the project's methodology at a U.S. Office of Education invitational conference, I was almost laughed off the podium. Good friends took me aside to warn that I needed to begin damage control immediately, for I might have ruined my career with my unscientific proposals. Unfortunately, I took their advice, tucked the paper in the bottom drawer of my file, and never listed it on my vita. But I could not expunge it from my belly; it festered there, and that uncomfortable feeling returned. How could something that I had found so useful, so evocative, and so impressive be that wrong?

During this same period I became well acquainted with David L. Clark, who left the Cooperative Research Program of the U.S. Office of Education to come to Ohio State as Associate Dean for Research. He was interested, as was I, in ways to produce change in education, and together, we developed what became known as the Clark-Guba Model of Educational Change (positivist modeling was still in my blood). But neither of us had been able to fully free ourselves from our shared latent belief structure. The notion that there could be developed a generalizable model of the educational change process still enthralled us. Needless to say, although it was widely implemented, the model never worked well, and that failure added to my visceral discomfort.

My head and my gut stagnated then for some eight years, during which time Clark and I moved to Indiana University in administrative roles. But in 1974 we abandoned them to undertake a national study of knowledge production and utilization (KPU was a buzzword of the time) funded by the Office of Education. We gathered information on the 1,367 university-level schools, colleges, and departments of education then extant, much of it via elaborate questionnaires (old habits die hard). While the masses of numbers that we massaged in our computers did produce some interesting normative findings, we felt that our best insights about the way research production and utilization were carried out came from some 20 site visits during which we observed actual programs in action and talked with the people implementing them. The tacit visceral rumblings began to take more propositional form.

I returned to teaching in the spring of 1977. A colleague, Bob Wolf, had some novel ideas about carrying out evaluation based on judicial (court) proceedings as a metaphor. Thanks to his influence, I first realized that there might be many models for doing evaluation. Bob called his approach "naturalistic," and I began to warm up to the possibility of pursuing evaluations, and even inquiries in general, in ways that differed markedly from the "scientific" approaches we had been accustomed to. It was hard to make a rational argument about why I thought the naturalistic approach was congenial, but it just "felt right."

I was fortunate to receive an invitation from the UCLA Center for the Study of Evaluation to spend the summer of 1977 as a visiting scholar. I was expected to write a monograph, but it could address any topic I chose. After consulting with Bob Wolf and two other colleagues,

Yvonna Lincoln and Barbara Tymitz, I decided to follow their joint advice and do a monograph on "naturalistic" evaluation, whatever that might turn out to be.

I had trouble sorting out my notions about this naturalistic evaluation; to help me in that process, I put together a table contrasting conventional and naturalistic approaches to inquiry in general. The table made such distinctions as logical positivism versus phenomenology as the philosophical base, verification versus discovery as the basic purpose (a distinction I later rejected), singular versus multiple reality manifold, unrelated versus relevant context, and so on. I found the list quite helpful, so I was rather surprised when my old Ohio State colleague Dan Stufflebeam accused me one night of having introduced a major schism into the profession. Why did I find it necessary to polarize these dimensions? Weren't intermediate positions possible? I was challenged to articulate more clearly what the differences were and to justify delineating them in such antithetical fashion.

Since I had a great respect for Dan, I was worried about his charge; it continued to eat at me for some months. I finally decided that he might be right, and I made a concerted effort to define middle positions on my dimensions that might lead to some compromise (my first and last attempt to make different paradigms commensurable). It was certainly the case that some of the dimensions could yield intermediate positions, but others, particularly that one dealing with the nature of reality, continued to be intractable despite my best efforts. I slowly came to realize what my gut had been trying to tell me for years: that there was an intrinsic problem with current modes of conceptualizing the world and defining ways to study it. My daughter Susan, then in medical school, called my attention to Thomas Kuhn's (1970) *The Structure of Scientific Revolutions*, and it all fell into place for me. I had been skirting the edges of a paradigm shift, whereas I should have been joining a revolution.

While the old visceral gnawing almost disappeared with that insight, it was soon replaced by new feelings of doubt, insecurity, and anxiety. I began to wonder whether I might be leading interested colleagues, and especially students, down a "primrose path," making it difficult for them to get jobs, to be published, or to be promoted and tenured in the face of the hegemony still enjoyed by adherents of positivism. The resistance was and still is formidable, but I have come to discount its influence heavily, noting with pleasure the increasing interest in and commitment to *some* alternative to positivism, as more and more individuals become convinced of the poverty of the received view. I now look forward confidently to a continuing revolution; it is too late for reactionary forces to subvert it.

During those periods when I experienced intuitive discomfort without being able to articulate why, I had typically been unaware of my "creative" processes (if they are properly called "creative") at the time of their occurrence. But I had been struck years ago by one construction about "stages" in the process of creativity, of which there were said to be four: preparation, incubation, illumination, and implementation. Proceeding from that base (perhaps illogically, since my essential idea purported to be a generalization), I began to build a metaphor to help me to understand myself. The telling of it to students and others interested in "how I got from where I was to where I am" has proved useful, according to their reports, and so I take leave to retell it here.

In this metaphor, I imagine a "little green man" who inhabits a securely locked room somewhere in my head (funny, since all my unease had been in the belly!). I cannot enter the room, but fortunately, the door has a kind of mail slot through which I can drop items of information, insights, and other relevant tidbits (preparation). I have no idea what the little green man does with them, but whatever it is, it requires some unpredictable amount of time (incubation). Sooner or later, however, he opens the door a crack and shouts, "Get to the typewriter" (he preceded the days of word processors and still operates on the old software). When I do, he somehow transmits to my fingers what I am to write, and it is frequently a surprise to me as I see the product roll out of the machine (illumination, or as Archimedes expressed it, the "aha" experience). It's up to me to do the implementation myself.

I have come to believe that human beings have unrecognized but available resources that are called into play (or should I say *realized*, i.e., made real?) whenever they face what appear to be unsolvable problems or irresolvable conflicts. As they mull those problems and conflicts, they become more than usually sensitive to ideas, insights, metaphors, and feelings they encounter in reading, in classrooms, on the job, in everyday conversations, in pursuing even mundane tasks, and in a myriad of other ways, most of which at first glance seem so irrelevant that they are hardly noticed. These materials are the items of information that are stuffed through the mail slot (the inputs). What the little green man "is," or how he "works" on these materials, is unknown (and probably unknowable; well, it's all a figment of my imagination—my imaging—anyway), although it surely depends upon the little green man's (my own?) present level of sophistication, among other things. But in all events his efforts are directed toward "making sense" of what is presented. Sometimes that task is easy and sometimes hard, and perhaps even undoable at that point in time.

For me the most important feature of this metaphor is that it treats the creative process as essentially tacit. It suggests that a human being is capable of many more things than he or she might be able to articulate, or, to coin a phrase, "There are more things in heaven and earth, Horatio,/Than are dreamt of in your philosophy." It suggests that one ought to be willing to "go with the flow," with one's feelings, not being too hasty to reject what cannot immediately be defended as rational. It suggests a willingness to suspend disbelief on those rare occasions when the cry to get to the typewriter is followed by output that seems to be completely at odds with what one had earlier believed, a willingness to trust that little green man.

This metaphor has meaning not only for the production of single ideas, or professional papers, or book chapters, but for the entire process of conversion that I tried to describe above. I have convinced myself that it is this little green man who, over decades, accumulated and organized the evidence and insights that were needed to "convert" me *away from* positivism. He gave me hints here and there (witness the critical incidents I have recalled above) until one day I realized—made real—the crucial insight that positivism rested on a system of beliefs no more foundational than any other, and therefore deserved no more privilege than any other. Examination of available alternatives then convinced me to convert *to* constructivism for the time being. I hope I can remain open to other alternatives that may be proposed in the future that are even better informed and sophisticated than my present choice.

Conversions have a time dimension. Some persons can be converted on first hearing the "good news" (as St. Paul apparently was on his road to Damascus), while others need a longer time. For me the conversion process was labored, and not at all appreciated during the time in which it took place. It was hardly conscious; it was visceral rather than rational. It needed the strong criticism of a trusted respected colleague to make me face the tough question of commensurability, which led, finally, to the realization that what was at stake was a revolutionary paradigm shift. The road to Damascus turned out not to be an easy one; there were many dead ends and U-turns. I got lost many times along the way. Instinct alone sometimes kept me going, that and the hope that just around the corner I'd be surer of the way to go—until I got lost again. I fervently pray that my little green man is still working, helping me to think through the many anomalies and inconsistencies that remain in my view.

I would be remiss if I failed to mention a major formative influence on my personal development that I have so far neglected. I have been fortunate to be joined both as a professional colleague and a life mate by Yvonna Lincoln, who has helped me see dimensions and entertain ideas that my early training as a scientist, mathematician, and statistician had largely obfuscated. While I have not always understood (and sometimes resisted) the challenges she set, the fact that she got ideas churning through my mind (a feast on which my little green man doted) has had a major impact. I am a better professional for it.

Of Life Real and Unreal

Lous Heshusius

I was late for my first class. It was only my second day on this particular campus and I had lost my way around. The class I had enrolled in was called "Learning Theories for Educators." It was in the mid-1970s, and I was taking my first graduate course at an American university. I had looked forward greatly to this next step in my educational career.

When I finally found the classroom, I was over half an hour late and the professor had already started. I settled myself in the back of the room, and focused on what he was saying. A story about, it sounded like, training rats to run through mazes. "Rats," my mind said, "I must be in the wrong building." I turned to the student next to me, pointing to the name of the course noted on the course outline, and whispered: "Is this the right class?" It was. Then my mind said (as it is our inescapable human need to make sense), "He must be talking about his hobby." Many of us have known professors who introduce themselves in the first class by talking about their families and their hobbies. Needless to say, at the end of the course we were still talking about rats and pigeons doing very strange and silly things to get a pellet of food into their half-starved bodies. (I also learned in that course that Skinner kept his rats at 80% of their normal weight—as well as isolated—and all I could think of during the rest of the course was the rather logical implication: Do we have to starve and isolate our children for this to work?)

I still vividly remember being dazed. I remember it as if it happened yesterday. The shock to my entire system was too great to ever forget, and I can trace the first impulse that led to a series of intellectual pursuits to discover the Why behind all of this to that very first class. Something was WRONG! I felt it, not as an intellectual analysis (which was not available to me at the time), but as a bodily/somatic experience: I was stunned. I could not follow what was going on. While everyone seemed busy taking notes, I sat there feeling completely isolated and confused. I remember having difficulty getting up from my seat at the end of class. My mind kept saying: This is not about education. What am I doing here? Yet everyone else around me seemed to act normal, as if nothing were wrong. Now I wonder if there weren't others who reacted as I did. But I was too stunned to raise any questions. The professor had lectured as if it were the most normal thing to talk about rats in a course supposedly dealing with people. (Epistemologically speaking, I learned later that the professor was perfectly correct from his perspective: The course was about rats and was supposed to be about rats. And yes, it was also about people's learning. What was the problem?)

In retrospect, things might have been a bit different for most students in that class. Most of them had their undergraduate training in the United States. I had attended teacher college in the Netherlands, where I grew up and where I had been nurtured on Piaget, Montessori, and anthropological and phenomenological approaches to education. I had taken for granted that a graduate course called "Learning Theories for Educators" would deal with education from similar perspectives but at a deeper level. Also, in the Netherlands, I had "successfully taught," as they say, at both elementary and secondary levels and also in special education. And I had managed to do so without any knowledge of ratology. On the day I signed up for that course, I entered a different world altogether, a world I would refuse to acknowledge as a more adequate one than the one I knew, a world shaped by an epistemology I would study and study and study until I could fashion an intellectual account of the reasons why I refused to accept it.

My particular background, then, makes me not quite the kind of person who shifted fundamental assumptions from a positivist worldview to a qualitative, interpretive one. I never believed in the former in the first place. I remember taking courses in experimental research and having to learn the classic Campbell and Stanley (1966) book on experimental design virtually by heart (by mind, rather, for the heart was surely not supposed to be involved) and thinking, "Wait a moment. If *I* were one of the subjects, I would not respond the way I would because of the experimental treatment, but because I am a woman, because I was reared in Western Europe, because I am a mother, because I like literature, because I felt tired that day, because I thought the experimental task meaningless, or intriguing, or a little absurd, because . . . because . . . because." I would raise my objections to the instructor, who would always say, "Well, you don't understand. Here is how you do it . . . " I would feel exasperated with his response, and only later, when I started to read the history and philosophy of science, did I learn that ignoring the Why question and replacing it with the How question is one of the quintessential characteristics of mechanistic thought. The instructor had learned it well.

As mandated, I went through all the traditional training in quantitative methods and experimental design, course after course, it seems, and also engaged in experimental research as a research assistant. Not happily so, for it required elimination of all knowing that occurred below my neckline, but it was the only game in town. It took about four years before I discovered that, in fact, there *was* an alternative.

Toward the end of my doctoral course work in the late seventies, I woke up one morning and suddenly realized with a shock that I had almost completed my course work in special education, knew everything there was to know (or so it seemed, looking at the piles and piles of books and articles accumulated over the years) about theories, models, testing methods, and research findings, but that I had no idea what people we put in institutions, for instance, thought themselves. What *did* they think about their lives? What made them sad? What made them happy? What were their wishes for the future? Did they think differently about life from the way we do? What did they think about their lives in institutions? How did they live there on a day-by-day, hour-by-hour basis? In all my courses and readings, I had not heard their voices. After I finished my degree, I might have been able to take a position of leadership in an institution, and I would not have known a thing about the residents, nothing about them as people. I then realized that learners in school did not fare much better. Not any better, in fact. Nothing in our courses had reflected the voices of youngsters in school, either. I suddenly felt that I had been on a sterile intellectual trip for five years in graduate school, having left real life and all that belonged in it behind. I had missed the real significance of the lives of those I thought I had learned so much about. I had learned nothing about *them*, and therefore nothing about myself. I had only learned rational constructions of them that were severed from real life, thereby distorting it, often in harmful ways. The realization that very morning brought a feeling of paralysis, a deadly tiredness, and a feeling of betrayal. The unreality of much of what I had learned suddenly haunted me. I remember getting dressed that morning, determined that I had to do something about it, although I did not know what could be done.

Luckily, I had one more seminar to take. And I'll forever credit Samuel Guskin, who taught the course, for handing me the solution. He brought in the now classic *The Cloak of Competence* by Robert Edgerton (1967), an anthropologist who had turned his attention to people who had been discharged from institutions for the retarded, to see how they were doing in their now "normal" lives. It was a qualitative, ethnographic study, the first of its kind in special education as far as I know, and my excitement knew no bounds. Here it was, real people, real lives, real knowledge. I was ready to do my dissertation.

From then on, my interest in the paradigmatic underpinnings of all we do started in earnest, a course of study I have found among the most fascinating in my life. But the intellectual life (which for me finally had started to focus on real-life meaning) and the day-to-day world (which in special education was still lodged in unreality) rarely go smoothly together. After completing my degree in 1979, I took a job that combined university work with the actual teaching of youngsters the school had labeled "learning disabled." It was my first job teaching in the special education system at an American public school. I could not believe the drawers full of "stuff" that were handed to me. Loads of programmed materials, workbooks, worksheets, filling-in-the-blank exercises, phonics exercises, all sharing one overwhelming characteristic: They were pieces of things. Pieces without any context, without any meaning. Unreal. This piecemeal approach to teaching and learning literally drove me just about out of my mind. Again, my memory of this confrontation is an intense bodily one: It was as if my heart sank into my stomach every time I tried to work with this "stuff." I would literally feel the pull of gravity and would feel a wave of something close to nausea go through me. Some years ago I actually published an article in which I referred in a very personal manner to that experience. I don't think I can express what I experienced better than I did then. Upon looking at all these instructional materials, I wrote:

> I would force myself to read it all, or rather not to read but to skim, for there was nothing to really read. I would get lost, then force myself to start over again, and I would invariably feel a tiredness, a sudden fatigue. I was not absorbing anything. My own mind had become a blank. Yet, I would tell myself: I need to use them, for weren't others doing so, and didn't all these publishers publish them, didn't theories support them, didn't I see them in curriculum laboratories and at instructional exhibitions? I would think of the students I had to teach the next day, and I would feel depressed, powerless, even desperate. For why would they want to learn something that was boring, that could not even hold one minute of my own interest, that made no sense contextually, that contained nothing a person wanted to learn? (Heshusius, 1984, p. 364)

I received dozens of letters in reaction to this article. One superintendent of special education requested 50 copies to give to all her principals and consultants, for, she said, I had verbalized what so many teachers had tried to tell her. I was surprised at the kind of feedback I received, and then I was not surprised. For I know that our somatic lives don't lie. We can try to repress what they tell us, but they will not go away.

I held that position for five years, during which time I became deeply involved in studying the historical evolution of the assumptions of the mechanistic paradigm that was so unacceptable to me. I had to understand where it all came from and why I was supposed to work as I was supposed to. I came to understand to some degree the deeper assumptions in which the system was grounded. But I was not prepared for the even greater absurdities that could happen under the paradigm's dictate.

Teaching under the guidelines of Public Law 94–142, I had to write behavioral objectives according to the interpretation of the law by the local state education agency. I was expected to write objectives such as: "By Christmas Ann will read a paragraph of five sentences with no more than three mistakes, four days in a row." As far as I was concerned, that was not the way to assess or plan for a student's education. It had nothing to do with good pedagogy; in fact, it stood in the way! I was fortunate that the principal of the school, an old-timer, could not agree more. The special education supervisor of the local state education agency, however, did not. I explained to him the pedagogical reasons why I could not possibly write such objectives and teach and assess according to their prescription, but to no avail. In the heat of our disagreements he angrily told me one day that he could take me to court for "civil disobedience" (!): I was violating PL 94–142! I gasped, and felt my body pulling back from him. I then heard myself say: "Okay, then, I will prepare myself well." The threat was never carried out. But the whole episode made it still more imperative to go on with great intensity and affection (the latter was difficult to do in the beginning), to try to analyze how it was possible that we had strayed so far that teachers had no ownership any more over anything and had to obey rules they found objectionable on solid pedagogical grounds. I use the word "affection" because if you engage in serious debunking, you had better do it in creative and high spirits, the kind that Stephen Gould (1981) refers to as "positive debunking," or what Jiddu Krishnamurti (1954, 1972) calls "creative discontent"; otherwise it may make you ill.

How do I end this story? A thought from one of my favorite writers, Ralph Waldo Emerson (in Richardson, 1990, p. 199), comes to mind: "People wish to be settled; only as far as they are unsettled is there any hope for them." I know he was right. To be so unsettled, shocked really, propelled me into a more complex view, and I have loved the journey, however difficult it has also been. And now I wonder about the sense of discomfort with what I am presently believing and doing in relation to my work, something . . . I can't quite articulate. But I feel it. It has started to become unsettling. I must wonder what the full story some 10 years from now will turn out to be. But this time, I will attempt to be more conscious of the process of change as it happens, and not doubt it for the wrong reasons. I am delighted that the (re)turn to interpretation and qualitative thought in educational research has made it easier to do so. We no longer are forced to pretend that the unreal life is real.

On Feeling Right:
A Paradigmatic Epiphany

NEITA KAY ISRAELITE

As a teacher of deaf children in the early 1970s, I was indoctrinated, without being aware of it, into a positivist-behaviorist worldview that seemed to have no end. Initially, what I taught, how I taught, and how I viewed the students entrusted to my care were influenced by theories and pedagogies in deaf education based on the deficit-driven medical model. However, difficulties began to arise when what I knew to be true from professors, supervisors, and colleagues did not match what I knew to be true from my own experience and in my own heart and mind. I offer the following glimpse of my life as a teacher during that time, when I was trying to deal with the notion of success as it applied to the students in my class.

I was working with deaf students, ages 9 through 12, who had spent many years in segregated oral communication classes in which they were permitted to use spoken English only. These youngsters had been labeled "oral failures" because of their obvious great difficulty in understanding and using speech. Some were also labeled "behavior problems," because of their difficulty in getting along socially in classes where spoken English was the only accepted mode of communication.

Our class, however, was a total communication class in which the students were encouraged, for the first time in their public school careers, to augment speech with signs and finger spelling. To my delight, they appeared to flourish as the year progressed. Their frustrated attempts to speak or use rudimentary gestures were replaced by a standard communication system. Imagine a 10-year-old girl with unintelligible speech requesting her favorite food for lunch — not by pointing or making guttural noises and gestures no one understood, but through a sign system; or a 12-year-old boy with a violent temper expressing his rage by signing an angry message instead of throwing tables and chairs. It was exhilarating to be part of a classroom where students were discovering the power of language and the excitement of learning.

These and other experiences were evidence to me of the significant progress these children were making. I knew they had begun to experience success personally, socially, and academically. The parents agreed with me, once they had recovered from the shock of receiving positive reports about children who had received almost exclusively negative reports in previous oral classes. Mary's mother said Mary was awake, dressed, and ready for school each day at least an hour before her bus was scheduled to arrive. John's parents were so impressed with his new and frequent attempts to communicate through sign language that they registered for sign classes themselves.

Unfortunately, it was hard for me to persuade some colleagues and the program supervisor of the changes I was observing. My vision of success held no meaning for them. Sometimes the children were so eager to participate that they could hardly contain themselves. I interpreted their enthusiastic behaviors (e.g., waving their hands and jumping from their seats in an effort to be called on) as a breakthrough. The program supervisor interpreted them as examples of my lack of control.

My knowledge of the students and their in-class progress was not considered sufficient criteria by which to judge success. The program supervisor was quick to point out that scores on standardized achievement tests were not significantly improving; reading remained difficult; and written language was still not clear and concise. I was encouraged (or shall I say directed) to incorporate more behavioral approaches, return to phonics teaching (even for profoundly deaf students with unintelligible speech!), and calculate the percentage of correct responses on prescribed tasks to support any further claims.

The frustration, dismay, and disillusionment I felt nearly 20 years ago are as real to me today as they were then. These feelings were accompanied by an overwhelming sense of failure and confusion. If the program supervisor was right, then I was wrong. But how could I be wrong when the children were doing so well? Then I must be right. But how could there be two rights?

The root of my confusion, I later came to understand, was my reductionistic belief that there was one truth and that it was my job to learn that truth and teach it to the best of my ability. I did not know how to resolve the conflict.

I then went on to graduate school, where I learned the underpinnings of what I had been told to do. I became well grounded theoretically in various versions of behaviorism and reductionistic ways of seeing the world. Because I was unaware of the existence of alternative theoretical models, to me there was no other way to approach pedagogy. I did not understand that I was caught within a worldview; I did not know there were other ways of constructing knowledge.

Something Didn't Feel Right

After finishing my studies, I enthusiastically took up my first university position. In my teaching, however, something wasn't right. I had begun to question the value of teaching preservice teachers to write objectives so their students could accomplish such diverse tasks as appreciating art, adding and subtracting numerals from 1 to 10, and demonstrating respect for the elderly — all with 80 percent accuracy.

Something wasn't right about my research, either. In writing up a study on teenage siblings of deaf children, I was advised to focus solely on results of psychological measures and structured interviews. This meant I was not supposed to include other material that I believed to be very important. For example, one young woman answered my interview protocol questions only with terse comments. Yet after the formal interview, she spoke eloquently and in great detail about her experiences as the sibling of a deaf child. There was no place in my formal research report for her story, even though I found it far more enlightening than test scores and responses to a preplanned interview protocol.

As an American university student in the late 1960s, I was familiar with the credo, "If it feels good, do it." What I was doing didn't feel good, but I did it anyway, and had one of my first articles — presenting nice, convincing hard data — accepted for publication.

Pizza and Monopoly as Metaphor

By the early 1980s, single-subject research design was in vogue. A colleague and I designed a study to teach deaf students to use metaphors through playing a form of Monopoly.

In the initial sessions of the study, the students eagerly participated. But even Monopoly gets boring after a while. The number of correct student responses plateaued, then diminished in inverse proportion to the rising summer temperatures and degree of disinterest. To ensure study completion, we introduced a new variable — pizza — to be awarded to all who kept up their level of enthusiasm and tried their best. We knew our students well. Visions of Pizza Hut put them back on track and saved the research. Or rather, since I now see that study as paradigmatically inadequate, pizza produced hard data that we could publish.

At the time, I was starting to have doubts about some aspects of the research. I believed we had taken a linear view of how language works. We had taught deaf students to use metaphors, but not to understand them. Later on, I recognized that we had shown them what to say, but not how to mean. I further realized that we had put ourselves in control of the students' learning by bribing them (spiced with pepperoni) into following our lead.

Pizza and Monopoly as metaphor didn't feel good, but I still did it. Lately, I have been trying to recall the reasons why I continued with this research: I wanted results; I wanted solutions. I wanted to publish; I had to publish. I liked treating the kids to pizza. I wanted a way to be able to "prove" the effectiveness of various teaching methods and interventions. Single-subject research design seemed to fit the bill.

As time went on, I became increasingly uncomfortable with what I was teaching and the kind of research I was doing. I was in a state of disequilibrium because there was dissonance between what I implicitly trusted to be right about teaching, learning, and research, and the nature of my practice. Yet, because of the philosophy of the department, there was no one within my milieu with whom to share my concerns or legitimize my feelings. I decided to start looking for alternatives that I intuitively knew must exist. It became crucial to me to feel good about what I was doing.

On Feeling Right

The changes I subsequently made involved accepting a new position at York University, moving to Canada, and being introduced to a holistic paradigm and qualitative research — alternatives I had been seeking.

As I began to read about and study holism and other nonobjectivist worldviews, I recognized that it is one thing to be able to understand and explain a paradigm, but quite another to make it your own and attempt to live your life by its tenets. Growing up and being educated within a reductionistic worldview has baked me into a mold, and I still find it hard to shake off those objectivist ties that continue to bind me.

Change is often gradual, but sometimes a certain event may occur that causes a sudden insight and speeds up the process. My paradigmatic epiphany occurred in 1992 as I was driving a colleague to her hotel at the close of a conference. To this day I can see us, riding down a busy Toronto street, heatedly debating our opposing views on education. I had been trying to explain a holistic, sociocultural perspective on learning and why I believe it offers a more adequate explanation than the traditional deficit model of what it means to learn differently from the norm.

Without resolving this issue, we shifted the conversation to research. I talked about my interest in qualitative research, my colleague about her latest quantitative investigation. She then urged me to try some psychological measurement studies; perhaps what she referred to as certain "personality deficits" noted in disabled children could also be found in deaf children.

As she spoke, I noticed that my hands were tightly clenched around the steering wheel, and despite the late summer heat, I felt a chill. At that moment, I realized that I could never again think of subjecting deaf children to measurement and quantification in support of the deficit model. Nor would I engage in research informed by the positivist paradigm any longer. My colleague and I lived in two different worlds.

I suddenly saw what it means to understand paradigms as ways of constructing knowledge in all that we do. Finally, I had arrived at that point where, in both theory and practice, the reductionistic-behavioristic worldview was no longer a successful picture of human behavior for me. I was ready to take the "imaginative leap beyond the walls of the positivist paradigm" (Kitzinger, 1990, p. 27). And I am still leaping.

Turning Doubting into Believing: Searching for Pedagogy Compatible with Life

MARY SIMPSON POPLIN

Ever since Lous Heshusius called me, I have been thinking about writing this personal essay. I have known deep inside that this will be an important experience, that the very writing of the essay will, in and of itself, cause more change to occur. I have worried about writing the essay because I know enough now to understand that at any point in my life there are so many things that are obscured from myself that will be interpreted or reinterpreted later. Then I have to ask myself, How do I really know how I have changed? How do I choose which stories to tell so that they may be helpful and not bore or burden the reader? How do I write about my transformation when indeed I am and always will be in the midst of it?

I will relate a few instances that, from where I stand now, seem to have been critical in my transformation thus far. For every event I describe there must be many others that may have been as significant. These events are all taken from my adulthood, but I must also say that I have a deep sense that my transition as an adult has in some significant ways been a trip back to things I knew as a child (perhaps not consciously) and lost along the way, lost partially in an education system that nurtured only my intellect, and only a narrow part of that. While I will speak here primarily about my professional journey, it is of course inseparable from my personal journey. The same struggles and joys exist in both. That I like to intellectualize everything and that I am in the academy is no accident. It is a problem of mine, personally and professionally, and one of the academy's. It is a problem we both perpetuate in the world. I'm sure that when I am done, it will be a problem with this text as well.

College actually captured and nurtured my intellectual leanings more than any previous schooling, and I did well in classes where I enjoyed the content and/or the professors. I loved special education classes and was enthralled with discussions of the brain and psychological processing. I was student assistant to a very compassionate special education professor. My secretarial skills were so bad that I was probably more trouble than assistance. She never complained.

With regard to her understanding of her field, this professor had become convinced that success with students with learning disabilities depended not on compassion and a sense of purpose, but on the correct diagnosis of and instruction in perceptual and psychological processing skills such as auditory discrimination and visual memory. I admired her and thus learned all I could from her, even things I was to have to unlearn, which in and of itself is an important lesson. When I began teaching, I tried all the things I had been taught and promoted them to wary colleagues. But then came the day when, driving with my friend Janine to the small town outside of Wichita Falls in Texas where we taught, we began talking about our doubts that teaching visual and auditory processing skills was improving our students' reading. Janine found the early research written by Don Hammill, which began to confirm our suspicions. Ah, science was on our side again, so we could move on to what then I thought was the opposite of psychological processing — behaviorism. We began gradually to supplant processing activities with what I thought was real reading, writing, and math. I thought the serious work of real reading was using the Merrill Linguistic Readers phonetically.

For fun I would have my class write stories, read books to them, grow plants, have ant farms, listen to music, build gingerbread houses, and go shopping for our own spelling words by walking around the block. I enjoyed these times immensely, but I never let myself think *this* was teaching. I knew nothing of whole language. I had been taught to teach "scientifically," and by then I had learned that lesson so well as to have become almost sufficiently indiscriminate. Feelings of guilt always sent me back to the text. I was sure the experts, who wrote the books I was reading and using, and those who had taught me, knew best. I felt that when I was not doing the official lessons I was just "playing" with the kids because I enjoyed the way their minds worked. I suspected that many of my colleagues also believed the same. That critical and scientized voice that sat on my shoulder then and said, "You are not teaching" still sits there occasionally. I noticed it again just last semester when I asked graduate students to read and discuss a novel a week (18 novels) written by people of color in order to immerse ourselves in multiple perspectives, rather than read only a few novels and write a paper. I felt that we needed an immersion in ideas that were foreign to many of us, and that most of us were not prepared to write on these topics. To do so would bring us to premature closure, make us think we had come to conclusions versus leaving us open to understanding our own limited experience in the world. But what kind of teacher in graduate school doesn't require a final paper or exam, I thought to myself.

I loved graduate school at the University of Texas, where quantitative research was being used to "scientifically" determine that the perceptual/psychological process model in learning disabilities was flawed, something I had already intuited. I loved the logic of it all. It was here, in the mid- to late 1970s, that I began my struggle to learn and then to resist behaviorism. It was here that I learned to conjugate millions of academic tasks into small behavioral objectives. At first, it resonated well with my desire for order and control. Here, also, Don Hammill, Steve Larsen, and Lee Wiederholt began to teach me to write and to argue. They were extremely generous. In retrospect, I realize that the most important gift from graduate school was the confidence that I could make it in the academy. This was no small feat for an overprotected and undereducated young woman from rural Texas.

My book with Steve Larsen (Larsen & Poplin, 1980) is a testament to what I learned intellectually and proof that I was a behaviorist once, or at least that I could write like one. It was probably the first book that really outlined curriculum-based assessment and instruction in special education. Even then I remember many moments of doubt as I developed objectives broken down into reductionistic skills. Especially troublesome and lame were my attempts to reduce social behaviors and larger concepts such as reading comprehension. I remember wondering why I seemed only to be able to break down mechanical skills and worrying that I had left unattended, or worse, poorly attended, the more important things. Was this all there was to schooling? I forged ahead with a very uneasy feeling. It was the last time I was to really look at curriculum scope and sequence in that way.

As I was leaving Texas for Kansas, things started to happen in my little circle. I was being introduced to the whole language movement and Piaget's constructivism by Kim Reid, Gaye McNutt, and Virginia Brown. I was intrigued. It sounded like home to me. Graduate students began to use some of the more holistic methods in the severe learning disabilities clinic that I directed at the University of Kansas Medical Center. I began to see my old classroom again as if for the first time and to learn, teach, and later write more about the whole language movement.

Also at Kansas, I became the editor of a research journal, *The*

Learning Disability Quarterly. That experience was to radicalize me, to send me, intellectually and emotionally, running away indiscriminately from all reductionistic explanations and practices. Ultimately, it sent me, with the help of Lous Heshusius, to study qualitative research. I had taught youngsters the public schools saw as learning disabled. I had enjoyed them as people. I knew college students who showed characteristics of learners we see as having "learning disabilities," and yet I could not find these people in the pages of the journal. All I could find, on page after page (some of them mine), were descriptions of little things that, statistically speaking, a group of people couldn't do, and rationalizations for why they should do these things. Although we were receiving close to 300 manuscripts a year, we were not receiving any evidence that all the considerable energy educators were spending on diagnosis and carefully planned instruction was leading to anything productive in the real lives of students with learning differences. And yet, I knew that those of us who wrote and studied about learning disabilities cared about these students' plight in schools. The last two years I was editor of *Learning Disability Quarterly*, I wrote a series of editorials that tried to describe my thoughts and concerns regarding the deficit-driven nature of the field of special education and, in particular, learning disabilities.

Later, while teaching at Claremont Graduate School, a group of us began to pursue research that demonstrated the nontraditional talents of the youngsters schools label learning disabled, and further challenged the deficit-driven nature of the field. First we had to develop or find assessments of nontraditional talents that would be appropriate for the students with learning differences. We decided to study this area initially in a quantitative manner so as to appeal to the most ardent supporters of reductionistic pedagogies. We are still in the midst of publishing this work.

I still remember the first time I said anything publicly about my emerging doubts regarding reductionistic practices. I was a member of a panel in 1980, and we were each to respond to something or other about strategies training. My mind was a blur; the only thing I could think of was a question — How would strategies training help students with learning disabilities in their lives after school? I asked the question and then I began to shake inside; I had nothing else to say. I didn't know the answer, I hadn't planned the question, and I don't know if anyone even heard it. But I said it and I remember shaking for a long time afterward. Then I wondered similarly, thinking of my own classroom full of young students not so many years before, What had I taught them, what good had it done for them? I had just begun to ask questions that would plague me for years to come.

Three years after going to Kansas, I visited Claremont for an interview. I spoke there of my emerging distrust of behaviorism and affection for holistic principles. Malcolm Douglass, longtime leader of The Claremont Reading Conference, which had always been opposed to reductionism, and his wife took me to dinner. I knew that if I was offered the job I would go, and I did. In Claremont, I was the only special educator, and I began to see that there was an academic world that was full and rich with ideas not present in my own field. I realized how frustrated and bored I had become. Bringing that world of ideas to special education became the focus of my work. At the same time, my interests expanded. I sought any and all nonreductionistic academic literature. I looked into new paradigms, constructivism, discrete mathematics, language arts, science, the new physics, feminist theory, qualitative research, and multiple intelligences. None of these had ever been a part of my formal education.

I began to notice experienced teachers and young intern teachers who had the sensibilities that it had taken me years to recognize. With like-minded colleagues, I began to try to construct a teacher education program that would nourish and deepen rather than diminish teachers' own intuitions and energy. In 1986, I turned my primary attention away from special education and began directing the teacher education internship program. I developed partnerships with public schools that eventually led to the establishment of The Institute for Education in Transformation, which I now also direct.

For a while I found a new home in feminist theory. It was here that I found philosophic and theoretical principles that differed dramatically from the logical positivist ones I had learned. Finally, I could see what I had learned so well and from where it had come. I could begin to see reductionism's multiple dangers not only in education, but in the world. I studied for two summers with Carol Gilligan and her colleagues at Harvard. I taught classes on women and education. Now I understand that these classes, too, were confused with the contradictions of feminist theory, which seeks to describe and validate the feminine side of human nature, and feminist politics, which, at least early on, encouraged women to emulate male values. Nonetheless, feminist theory has had a profound effect on my work.

John Rivera at Claremont Graduate School was the first and most significant colleague to encourage and help me move toward an understanding and appreciation of other cultural perspectives. I am sure these non-European perspectives will be some of the most critical factors in my own continued transformation. I also believe that this is the most important task for all of us in the world today. I am tremendously limited by my own monocultural and monolingual nature, and my limitations effect everything and everyone I touch. I still find myself attracted to Cartesian splits and logical rationalizations. I strongly suspect that what I, and others, have called the new paradigm is not new at all, and that it is only my own personal and cultural limitations and racism that led me and other Euro-Americans to think it was new in the first place.

I began to study other anti-reductionistic, anti-racist intellectual movements such as critical, liberatory, feminist, and multicultural pedagogies; ethnic studies; qualitative research methods; critiques of the white feminist movement; and the work of Chicano, Black, and Asian scholars, poets, and novelists. I have been strongly influenced by the work and life of Paulo Freire. I also continue to learn from students and colleagues of color, who have been extremely generous. I have begun to learn, teach, and write about liberatory and critical pedagogies, about monoculturalism, biculturalism, bilingualism, and participatory research.

My theories were all coming together nice and neatly . . . and then it happened, an experience I have still not sorted out. It happened when I went back to the classroom every morning during the spring semester of 1991 and taught English as a Second Language to a class of immigrant teenagers. Although armed with all the theories and practices collected over the past 15 years, I felt I had barely begun to understand enough to teach. I began to recognize more clearly that old voice on my shoulder that scolded me when it thought I was not teaching, and I started at last to doubt its message and believe my own. I have begun to understand that each of the pedagogical theories I studied and wrote about (constructive, critical, and feminist) are useful in their own time and place, and when used together, yet each are inadequate when applied ideologically and singularly.

Other questions began to plague me. I began to be fascinated by the way in which the high school students and I knew each other before the bell rang each morning and became estranged from one another after its call. I was both invigorated and exhausted every morning when I left after two short hours. I was appalled at remembering the feeling after a bad day, the amount of energy it took to turn myself around, the importance and difficulty of apologizing to students, the trouble I had in going with their conversations, and the ignorance I felt for being monolingual. I remember the frustration of our having only 50 minutes a day to build a community. I began to see more clearly how school was not structured for their lives or their education, but rather for a technological, quick-fix society in which education isn't designed to be serious. It wasn't structured for my education, either, but because of my other privileges (being white, English speaking, middle class, and situated well inside the dominant culture), I survived and in some ways profited from what is a bad experience for many.

During the time I was teaching in this urban high school, I had been writing three chapters on three different pedagogies—constructivism, critical, and feminist. I remember frequently asking myself which of the principles from these would be most helpful. There were three—Paulo Freire's notion that education should be both rigorous and joyous; the notion in feminine pedagogy that one must be authentic—not authoritarian or humanistic, but authentic; and the importance of community stressed by critical pedagogy. I tried increasingly to discover and expand on the students' "important questions" in a way that would allow us to relate as humans who are able to inspire one another. If the truth be known, it was much more difficult than it would seem, not because of the things we worry about in teacher education, such as content, curriculum, or teaching methods, but because of the emotional and physical aspects of relating to a large number of people at once, involving conflicting emotions such as compassion and irritation, eagerness and resistance, and inspiration and boredom. Teaching is so much more complicated than one can be prepared for. It is a neverending struggle of joy and frustration.

I knew things about teaching even as a young teacher that I was unable to articulate, things that were never validated in the academy or in the system when I started teaching, things that still aren't in the teacher education program I now struggle to make more responsive. For me, teaching always began with the forming of relationships that allowed us (students and myself) a point of departure, a place firmly grounded in a kind of understanding and respect for one another. From this common point we could move on to learn from one another. We moved at different rates and learned different things. We were free to explore, to concentrate, to fail and try again, in essence, to be human. I surmised that in relationship, in community, we could learn the things we needed and wanted to know. And what we needed to know, I thought, were largely the tools of life: reading, writing, and arithmetic. Today I still start with relationship, but I have become more concerned about what exactly constitutes the tools of life. I want broader cultural and social understandings to be represented in my teaching. I am more concerned with goals that go beyond the intellectual, and more concerned that the growth I promote is also healthy and inspiring. I want my classes to be about the important things in life, things important to my students and to the world.

It was through my recent experience teaching in a high school, through forming partnerships with schools and watching teachers work and grow, that I came to suspect even more profoundly that the problems of education had not been named. I knew the problems would have to be named inside the classroom by teachers and students and not by the academy, business, the media, or the politicians and policymakers, as has typically been the case. So for almost two years, in a participatory research process I designed with Joe Weeres, teachers, students, custodians, parents, aides, principals, and counselors talked about the problems of schooling. The first year's conversation from inside four public schools is contained in a report, *Voices from the Inside* (Poplin & Weeres, 1992). These conversations are filled with issues not taken seriously by the academy or by the formal structure of schooling. They include the primacy of relationships in learning and teaching; the ever-present racism in our society, in our schools, and in our hearts; the often avoided or distorted conversations about values and diversity; the boredom inherent in most formal education experiences; the fear we have of one another; the poverty of the physical environment of schools; and the despair we all feel when we see we are unable to do what needs to be done, as well as the hope that follows honest dialogue with one another. I have not even begun to sort through all these lessons, yet I know they indicate that the issues of schooling in America are profoundly moral ones. I also know that because achievement is the consequence of these moral issues and not the cause of its own problem, that achievement cannot be increased by working solely on achievement. My experience in this project as well as my recent high school teaching serve to remind me of how many questions still lie in wait for us to stumble upon. And sometimes the knowledge of my own struggle to understand paralyzes me and makes me want to stop talking and writing. It makes me feel as though I am just a part of the noise that all of us must stop listening to in order to find ourselves and one another. And on the other hand, some days it makes me want to write more quickly, speak more loudly, and listen more intently.

I have been a good academic. I have learned to doubt and to challenge and to critique. I am not required to believe. I have gone from ideology to ideology. I have succumbed to the logical positivist notion of opposites and their irreconcilability. I have tried to meld theories together. I have promoted "best" methods where there are none. I have rejected outright all reductionistic explanations when I shouldn't have. I have lived in my head and encouraged others to. And while I have not spared my intellect or my emotions in my work, I have denied that part of me that is most discerning and most unlikely to go off on a tangent unrelated to life. I am at a point where I feel I have enough new questions and have recognized enough important misconceptions that I am ready to take another leap in my own personal and professional journey. And now I am remembering from before that the most difficult part of change is not learning new things, but shedding old ones. I am ready now to search for a pedagogy compatible with life.

From My Either/Or to
My Both/And World

William C. Rhodes

Beginnings

My shift away from the classic scientific view of reality as a knowable "thing" "out there," and knowledge as a literal recording of it, was a gradual process. I didn't go to sleep believing in an objective, separate reality, and then suddenly and dramatically wake up in a new morning of disbelief. Shaking off the belief that my personal being, my experiences, my passions, my very life is bounded by the envelope of my skin was, and still is, not easy. How I merge into the world and how the world merges into me is still a puzzle—a booming, buzzing confusion, as William James, the psychologist, has described it.

In my professional life I developed first as an experimental psychologist, and then in my doctoral training, as a child clinical psychologist with a strong experimental bias. In spite of all the vicissitudes of my career, at heart I remained an experimental psychologist, a son of classic pre-20th-century science. My first writings as a psychologist were about human behavior modeled after laboratory rat behavior. They dealt with reshaping behavior in children who were emotionally disturbed.

Learning, rather than perception or the sociocultural life of the child, was my original passion. I believed strongly that learning was the source of emotional problems in the children I was drawn to. "Sickness," whether the psychological pathology of emotional disturbance or the social pathology of delinquency, was my abiding interest. My model was the conditioning-induced abnormal behavior of Pavlov's dogs and the learned neuroses of rats and a variety of other animals, produced in experimental laboratories across the world. It helped me understand how traumas in children's lives laid down "traces" that they carried through life. Gradually, I gravitated away from Clark Hull's "stimulus-response-reward" reflex theory to the broader view of E. C. Tolman, who demonstrated learning as composite "maps" of the world developed gradually inside the child's "mind" or "brain." But it was still a clockwork metaphor of the human condition. This was my truth, the absolute truth, at this point in my professional life. In my undergraduate work, my minor area of study was sociology. So it was natural, when I began my doctoral studies in clinical psychology at Ohio State University, that I should gravitate to the mentorship of Julian Rotter, who was writing and researching his famous clinical theory of socially learned behavior. There was also some lesser influence from George Kelly, who was the director of the clinical program, and who was developing his now-famous theory of the "personal construction" of reality, or the theory of "personal constructs." I found his theory and the research of his students quite fascinating, but I was much more drawn to social learning theory. George Kelly, who published his two-volume opus in 1955, was more or less ignored by American psychology during most of his life because his theory was seen as too "philosophical" and not fitting the positivist science worldview so dear to American psychology's heart. Now he has a worldwide reputation in many fields, including psychology, and is celebrated as an early constructivist. Although impressed, I did not follow his work and that of his students after graduating. Nevertheless, the yeast of his personal construct psychology must have been working in the deeper levels of my thinking.

My Professional Shaping

At this point, I must digress and talk about what led to my choice of profession and my transformation in the profession. From my earliest life, until after I was married and in the army in World War II, I had been determined to be a writer. I had modest success, such as my own radio program, reading poetry, including my own, to musical accompaniment. I also had some success in placing fiction and nonfiction pieces in small magazines. I was particularly proud of having had articles accepted in the *Atlanta Journal* Sunday Magazine Section, the training ground for Margaret Mitchell, Tess Crager, and other successful authors. When I was living in New Orleans, Gwen Bristow, whose novels were popular in the pre–World War II era, had helped and encouraged me in my writing.

Even after I married, while in the army, I had planned a career as a writer. However, during my five-year World War II service, first as an enlisted man and then as an officer in the medical administrative corps, I came into contact with several psychologists and psychiatrists. My secret opinion was that they were all a little crazy themselves, but I was fascinated with their theories of human behavior.

On Saipan, I was an adjutant, the assistant to a commander of a hospital for "battle fatigue" casualties. I was quite intrigued with these patients, and enrolled in several correspondence courses in psychology from "stateside" universities. This was the beginning of my study of learning theories, which was the total extent of experimental psychology at that time.

During the same period, while overseas, I began writing a novel about becoming "rock-happy" in the South Pacific. This was a strange malady that overcame almost all soldiers who spent more than six months on the Pacific islands. They became lethargic, detached, disinterested, uninvolved, semi-alcoholic—showing general personal deteriorations, and deviant or even bizarre behavior. To me, the battle fatigue patients in our hospital seemed to demonstrate only a more advanced stage of the rock-happy syndrome.

After returning stateside, following the fall of Japan, I took my partially finished novel to a publisher through a New York friend I had soldiered with overseas. Although I did not win a contract, again, as before the war, I received considerable encouragement regarding my writing talent. However, since I had married before going overseas, and since we had a child while I was in the South Pacific, I was faced with a major decision. I could risk having my new family become a satellite of a promising but impoverished author, or I could go to college and become a secure, socially acceptable professional.

The only reason I am bringing my aborted writing career into the picture is that I feel it had something to do with my much later quantum leap into the new paradigmatic view of reality and epistemology. My early experience prepared me to become a postmodern scientist, interpretivist, and transformed educator much later in life.

In most of my professional career I was grounded in classic science and pedagogy. I believed throughout this period that, as C. P. Snow had put it, there were two worlds in which I could choose to live. There was the rational world of reality—classic science's world of matter. Then there was the irrational world of fantasy—the unreal world created by artists and writers. I never dreamed that those two worlds could come together for me in a single, unified reality.

So very definitely, at that critical post–World War II juncture, I had to choose—writer or scientist. I chose science. I was a fully grown man with responsibility for a family. I had to choose the traditional fork in life. The road to writer was through an unmarked, irrational thicket, with an unmarked social result. The road to psychologist was along a clearly marked path, with absolute signposts—A.B., M.A., Ph.D.

Strange what a shift in worldview can do to reality. Like the simple turning of the eyepiece in a kaleidoscope, a shift of view reassembles the pieces of the world into a remarkable new mosaic. The postmodern worldview, which came to me late in life, brings all the pieces of reality into one—both scientist and writer, not either/or. It is like the meltdown of the caterpillar into a butterfly inside the cocoon.

The True Scientist

But I am getting ahead of my story. I first had to go through my original transformation after getting out of the army, to change direction and become a scientist instead of a writer. It meant turning from my enriched fantasy life. It meant separating the world from its entanglements with my emotions, my passionate engagements with reality. I had to extract my ego, and put the world "out there" where it belonged. When I thought about it at the time, I had to become a disciplined, objective observer, a spectator scientist, viewing the world for what it was, not what I felt it to be.

This was a very difficult transformation. I had realized long before that I lived in a world of fantasy, of deep personal interpretations of the world. I was also a strong social critic. I had early understood that everything I expected of the world was too much, too big. I realized that the world could not be the way I expected it to be just because I wanted it that way. That was why I had originally chosen the path of a writer—to live in the world of my own creations, to make my fantasies real and acceptable to other people. Now that I had chosen the path of science, I had to work my way from "inside" myself to the "outside" real world—the world of science. I had to give up the richness of my inner life for a more barren but more "accurate" reality. I had to put my creative tendencies on hold, and build a new self—a man of science. I made a conscious and deliberate effort to take on this new persona, an almost alien, objective persona.

Fortunately for me, psychology was considered by most only a "quasi-science." It was not anchored in matter. Also aiding my transition was that, much to its chagrin, psychology also harbored a branch that was oriented to people's life stories, filled with treacherous emotions, irrationalities, needs, and inner turbulences. It was the "unscientific" field of dynamic, clinical psychology. Here, the chaos of selves lived side by side with the lawfulness of the natural order.

While enjoying dynamic psychology, it was in the animal laboratory that I could truly feel like a "real" scientist. The chimpanzee, the dog, and the rat gave me the necessary distance. The animal lab gave me the privileged world of science in all its spectator purity. It gave me the world free of my inner self, my subjective mentality. The lower animals gave me a crystallized model of our own reactions to the "outside" world. I saw human adaptation in action. At the same time, however, I felt that I was sacrificing part of myself to achieve such clarity of what the world was, supposedly, really like. However, my clinical training, at the internship level, helped me resolve this conflict. From Freud and my clients, I learned the Reality Principle—Adapt to it, or go crazy. The inner neurotic program, I had learned, could be clearly created in the experimental laboratory, where stimulus-response-reward manipulation of animals mimicked the neurotic human condition. I could see neurosis being created in animals in front of my eyes. Now I had another, more personal reason for becoming a scientist. I would cure my writer self of its neurosis by strengthening my objective side.

The Ecological Factor

Again, however, my sociological minor, both in my undergraduate and my doctoral programs, had its influence on my career.

My experience in community medicine in public health and my training at Ohio State led to my own theory-building in ecological psychology. When I brought this framework to a national demonstration project for reeducating emotionally disturbed children, I was not aware that it was affecting me as well as the children. Without realizing it, a subtle shift had begun in my scientific worldview. By this time in my psychological career I had begun to envision life as a human/nonhuman network of interchanging systems. The sickness image of children who were disturbing to school and society dropped out of my thinking repertoire entirely.

I began to conceive of and celebrate child deviance as the preservation of an open, evolving human ecology (Rhodes & Tracy, 1974a, 1974b; Rhodes & Head, 1974). In my mind, there was still a subject–object distinction between person and physical environment, even though both were open rather than closed systems. Nevertheless, I still "knew" that the physical world could definitely influence the basic matter of the human mind, whereas the human mind in no way influenced the basic matter of the physical world. This was the underlying texture of reality. Matter was still privileged. Knowledge derived from direct, pristine contact with the physical world was still privileged knowledge. Matter-based truth was the ultimate truth.

Preparing to Turn

The classic experimental model was still my ideal for unveiling basic reality. My world was absolutely centered on a beautiful order and organization that existed "out there" — apart from me — in no way subjected to my view or my existence in it. I had not yet encountered quantum weirdness or John Bell's strange, nonlocal reality, which would later rip my assured scientific foundation from under my feet.

But unaware as I was, cracks had begun to appear in my subterranean armor. On the surface of my self-regard, I was still the consummate scientist-professional, but my growing ecological perspective was beginning to undermine my secure observer stance, my patiently constructed self-edifice. My very early contaminations of reality with passionate self-projections began to seep back and erode the cleavage between self and world, physical reality and metaphysics. Me and not-me was not as clearly delineated as it had been when I moved from literature to science.

Unknowingly, in my human ecology perspective, the world was an undivided, multifaceted whole; but I had to wait for my unexpected contact with the physics revolutionaries — Einstein, Bohr, Heisenberg, Schroedinger, and others — to have my solid material world drop out from under me. The book by Davies and Gribbin (1992), *The Matter Myth*, expresses more clearly than anything where I am today.

The present story conveys my internalization of new paradigm studies, which allows the final erasure of the line between science and literature, science and art.

In the fourth volume of the child variance series (Rhodes, 1975) on emotional disturbance, I had already come to understand multiple realities, but I had not yet started to articulate the postmechanistic, postmodern view of reality that is part of me today.

The World Has Changed

I now know that there can be no pristine sensory contact with a substantive world. As philosophy now construes it, there can be no immediate "presence," no direct contact with reality apart from our constructions of it. I don't know why I had never fully realized it before. I had intensely studied perception and cognition, particularly as seen through the frameworks of Piaget (1986) and Vygotsky (1987). I knew that perception was guided by inner illuminations, that sensation was informed by theory. George Kelly had planted the seeds of the personal construction of reality way back in my early days as a budding clinical psychologist.

However, all these tacit understandings had to wait for the impact of the New Physics upon me to make me take the leap into the new world — a world without substance, without local causality, without determination, a world mirroring all the unclarity and imperfections of myself, a world in which order and chaos reciprocate. It is a world in which science and art, me and not-me are one confluent stream, in which the flow forms eddies that, from a distance, separate the me in the stream from the not-me; but on close inspection, the flow and the eddies are a single stream.

As the bastard son of science and art, I have been legitimated because science has suddenly become literate. And although I cannot fully comprehend how the world is me and I am the world, I understand that all is connected, and all is one. I know that what I do and what I say is important and makes a difference in the world; and so I must be careful how I say it as I help make it exist.

Notes on Being an Interpretivist

Thomas A. Schwandt

Lous and Keith asked me to write a personal story about what it was like to do my work having "shifted fundamental epistemological assumptions" from a "quantitative, positivist tradition to a qualitative, interpretive one." I can't write that kind of travel story. I can't write it because I never had a road-to-Damascus kind of experience. You know, walking down the empiricist highway, seeing a blinding light of revelation, realizing that you've been in the grip of the dark side, changing one's self, that sort of thing. There has been no such turnabout or transformation in my being. But I think I have a story to tell about coming to be a teacher-scholar who works within an interpretive frame of reference.

On the Road to Graduate School

Once upon a time, I went to college thinking I would be a chemist. I liked science and math in high school and had won an award at a state science fair for what I recall was some bizarre fruit fly study that involved using a homemade gas chromatograph. I suppose that years of watching Mr. Wizard on television had somehow made a mark. I went to a liberal arts college and did the well-rounded education, but started piling up hours in chemistry and math. In my junior year, I had the opportunity to enroll in an overseas study program. It wasn't exactly what aspiring chemistry majors did, but at the time it seemed like a good idea to me. So off I went to live in Cambridge, England, for six or seven months. The tutors we had there in literature and art history exposed my romantic side, I suppose. I wandered the path of Wordsworth and Shelley and Keats, and I still have many of my poetry books, dog-eared and all marked up with annotations. I returned with an early complete edition of Shakespeare's plays and sonnets that now sits prominently displayed in our library. In short, I came back to the States feeling like a poet, gave up the rest of the work in chemistry, and took all literature classes. I made plans to go to graduate school in English literature.

However, it didn't really much matter what I had majored in because the year I graduated, I was picked high in the draft lottery and got my letter to report for a physical and induction into the Army. Westmoreland still needed a few good men to bomb, rape, destroy, and pillage the Vietnamese, and as luck would have it, I was one. For a variety of reasons, not least of which I found killing to be a really bad idea, I wasn't about to join up. Options were limited. I couldn't go to Canada because my dad had died not long before I was drafted, and my mom and brother needed me. I had a buddy headed for seminary, and he suggested that I apply because that might at least buy me some time to think. Since I was within six weeks of taking up a new home in the Southeast Asian jungle, that sure seemed like a good idea to me. By the fall after graduation, I was enrolled in seminary and working with the American Friends Service Committee on obtaining a conscientious objector deferment. It took so long to get that all worked out with my draft board—the one time I have actually found bureaucracy to be a good thing—that I never did have to salute and the war wound down to an end without me.

In seminary, I studied systematic theology and process philosophy and learned about hermeneutics and moral theology. I really enjoyed my time there, but never did finish my degree. For a few years after leaving seminary, I bounced around. For a brief time, I worked as a land surveyor and as a lab assistant in an environmental laboratory. I started teaching mathematics, chemistry, grammar, and composition in federal manpower development programs and postsecondary vocational school. Teaching really appealed to me, and I became interested in the issues underlying the manpower training and vocational programs in which I was working. I decided to go to graduate school to study education and manpower development.

Yet it wasn't long after I arrived at graduate school that I found the vocational education program lacking in many ways. There was lots of interest in measuring and testing, developing behavioral objectives and competencies, designing curricula to enhance skills, trait and factor theories, delivery systems, cost-benefit analyses, and the like. Frankly, I found it socially conservative and lacking an intellectual challenge. I was more attracted to the philosophy of vocational education, its role in the political economy, and so on, but those weren't major concerns of the folks I was working with. I stayed with it for about two more years, taking courses and doing several kinds of survey and interview studies, recognizing that I needed to move on. But, as you might guess if you are following the plotline thus far, I didn't have a real clear plan.

In the fall of 1978, I wandered into an experimental course called "Naturalistic Inquiry in Education" (there was no such creature on the books at the time) taught by Egon Guba, who, I would soon learn, had just finished his monograph *Toward a Methodology of Naturalistic Inquiry in Educational Evaluation* (Guba, 1978). This was different. In the course, Egon elaborated on the ideas presented in the monograph. He spoke passionately about the failure of experimental methodology in educational inquiry. In his lectures he wove a tapestry of terms I had never heard surrounding the methodology of an alternative kind of inquiry.

He often said that his own shift in beliefs about inquiry was a conversion experience. I found it all very interesting and exciting. I was intrigued by and drawn to the man's obvious passion for ideas and his critique of what appeared to be a not very useful way of examining human activity, although I recall not being very clear at the time on what all the fuss was about. But from that moment on, I embarked on the study, which continues to this day, of the nature of disagreements among different methodological and epistemological commitments in the social sciences.

Through participation in an informal group of graduate students and faculty that Egon organized, I began to learn more about how students, at least, perceived the tyranny of the experimental method and quantitative measurement and analysis in their fields. They recounted tales of open and strong opposition on the part of their advisers to any alternative ways of conducting educational inquiry.

Simultaneous with my studies with Egon and the late Bob Wolf in program evaluation, I took about 30 hours of coursework in statistics, measurement, and experimental design as part of my work in inquiry. If "they" were the enemy, as so many folks seemed to think at the time, then I figured I'd better know what "they" were up to. In those courses, I encountered the occasional obviously inane bid to measure just about anything and silly quarrels over precision in tests of hypotheses that themselves were never very precise. But I never felt that studying concepts and operations surrounding highly specified research designs or statistical analyses of data was a useless, meaningless, or, worse, abhorrent exercise.

Computing different kinds of statistics and crafting various types of designs was all sort of a game, playing with new tools. And I think I was pretty good at using the tools, although I haven't used them since. I have also learned since, as the economist Ely Devons pointed out many years ago, that there are striking similarities between the role of these tools in our society and some of the functions which magic and divination play in so-called primitive society. But I wasn't thinking like that then. When I took these courses, I didn't experience epistemological discomfort; rather, my troubles stemmed from wrestling with unfamiliar computer programs and mathematics. I remember spending long hours punching cards in the computer room and cursing my algebraic errors.

I know now that I didn't learn very much in these methods courses about issues of methodological commitment. Or maybe I did and I didn't. I did learn that these teachers of the so-called quantitative approaches had strongly held views about what made for "good" research. They were true believers in the value of parsimony, measurement precision, the statistical tests of hypotheses, the logic of experimental and quasi-experimental design, and so on.

But the commitment struck me as being largely one-dimensional and unreflective. These folks were committed to the efficacy of a set of methods, but I don't recall much, if any, talk in these courses about what one was committing oneself to when claiming that these were important things to do and important ways to know about human beings. That was the kind of talk in Guba's course and a few others, but not in these quantitative inquiry classes. There was no discussion of what we might be assuming about the aims of the social practice of inquiry when we chose to investigate the world using these tools. If anything, teachers in these courses were somewhat disparaging of these kinds of questions. I often felt that I was being taught that these questions didn't belong in these courses on methods.

At least since my days in Cambridge, questions about meaning, and about what the world must be like so that we can know it, have been important questions to me, so I started to pursue them in other ways. Rekindling the flames of a smoldering interest in philosophy, I took a minor in philosophy of science. I hoped to develop a view of how the paradigm quarrels that I was learning about in educational inquiry fit into some larger scheme of ideas about what it means to know. That work, coupled with ongoing discussions with Egon and professors in my minor area, started to give me something that I could sink my teeth into. Soon thereafter, with Egon's guidance, I began assembling all my work in order to qualify for a Ph.D. in inquiry methodology.

A significant signpost in the early days of that effort was the writing of a qualifying paper in inquiry methodology for submission to Egon and the faculty. I wrote (with what I now recognize as incredible temerity) a paper that was critical of the whole naturalistic approach to inquiry that Egon was advocating. That paper was the product of an effort to reconcile insights from the new philosophy of science with some of the claims of naturalistic inquiry concerning the nature of reality, the relationship between subject and object, a holistic-inductive approach, and so forth. It bothered me that there was a considerable body of thought about these issues that I felt wasn't adequately reflected in statements of what many were calling the new "qualitative paradigm." I thought then (and still believe) that we ought to get our story clear; that we shouldn't play fast and loose with concepts such as causality, positivism, and realism (and the latest watchword, "constructivism"); that we ought to stop insisting that the positivists were realists; and so on. I probably did not do a very good job of explaining that stance in the paper, but Egon accepted it graciously nonetheless. He even went me one better by urging me to continue my exploration of the kinds of epistemological and methodological issues underlying his work and the growing interest in qualitative methodologies in education more generally.

Another taking-stock point on the journey was my dissertation, foreshadowed in the qualifying paper. It was a very personal undertaking. It wasn't an autobiographical, this-is-my-life and I-once-was-lost-but-now-I'm-found story. Rather, it was personal in the sense that the dissertation was a way for me to work through the issues that I saw separating the so-called qualitative and quantitative folks and to come to some kind of resolution. I explored the kinds of commitments one was making in each case. I felt that much of the fuss was wrongly about method and procedure, when in fact it was a matter of arguing about different ways of knowing and being. I never found a resolution—in fact, I learned that there wasn't likely to be one—but I better understood the differences between competing worldviews.

In the dissertation, I made a claim (but not much of an argument) that choosing to inquire in a certain way and to hold a certain set of beliefs about human action was a moral as well as a cognitive commitment. In this context, the notion of *moral* means that such choices reflect beliefs about the way the social world should be and the way one ought to live. My work since then focuses on that issue in various ways. In the years since graduate school, I have continued to learn about various intellectual traditions underlying interpretive work and the kinds of commitments they promote. I have also continued to study theories of evaluation practice as well as practice the craft of program evaluation. My work since then also has taken me into the field to do a variety of case studies of educational programs and classrooms.

Postgraduate School Discoveries

It wasn't until I left graduate school and took up residence in the academic world as a teacher-scholar that the full force of the catechisms of different believers really hit me. With one exception, in each of the academic positions I held, I found myself in departments of educational psychology, surrounded by folks who were thoroughgoing empiricists and neobehaviorists. I often encountered situations in which colleagues would ask me to defend interpretive work and what I was about as if I were appearing before the Spanish Inquisition.

I recall that as a newly minted Ph.D. I gave a colloquium on qualitative methodology at Southern Illinois University to a group of clinical and educational psychologists. It was a total disaster as far as I was concerned. I was repeatedly pushed to fit interpretive thinking into an experimentalist and psychometric frame; I was called upon to explain what was wrong with reductionism, why a manipulative theory of causality was inadequate, why we should admit as research a seemingly totally subjective interpretation of an event, and so on. I learned how much I didn't know. I could talk the talk, but I knew far too little about important issues.

I was frustrated and angry, partially because I wasn't equipped to handle seasoned attacks. But I also was frustrated because I began to realize that this encounter wasn't simply (or even) about matters of methodology, it was about the politics of method. An orthodoxy was in place, and I was perceived as throwing stones at the temple (I don't think many that I threw did much damage that day). Folks seemed genuinely threatened by claims that there were alternative ways of knowing.

Over time, I have become less angry and a little bit smarter. As I write this, I sit in my office in a wing of a building occupied by educational, counseling, and school psychologists. They are good colleagues, but there are times when I feel like a stranger in a strange land. We often see the world so very differently. I tend to spend my time with colleagues interested in philosophy, history, and literature. The lenses through which they think about what it means to know our fellow human beings, what schooling, teaching, and learning mean, and so forth, seem, to me at least, to be more inviting, broader, more ecumenical, and more in keeping with my own. They seem to have little problem understanding that the sociopolitical world is, in one important sense, a world of our own making and that there are many legitimate ways of making sense of that world. In their way of looking there is room for testing, and measuring, and experimenting to learn about ourselves, but no illusion that it is the only or the best way we can do so.

I'd like to believe that encounters with the rear guard—with folks who cling to a one-right-way of doing social and educational research—are far less frequent now than they were a few years ago, and I prefer to think that is so because alternative forms of inquiry are gaining wider credence and popularity and because the guard is shrinking in number. Yet we still have a lot of scientism to overcome. I still am privy to horror stories from students who recount tales of being told that interpretive work is worthless, lacks rigor, and so forth; that they won't get a job doing these kinds of studies; that it's okay to do this kind of work after you've first established yourself by doing some serious quantitative work, and other such nonsense. I find lots of evidence of students having to justify qualitative studies by means of empiricist criteria and being forced to fit qualitative work into standard research reporting formats. It truly pains me to listen to students try to cope with such absurdity from their professors and fellow students.

The Present Moment

Never having really cashed in on that high school fruit fly experiment and thereby missing what might have been a career as the new Mr. Wizard; having spent time in England studying poetry and literature and learning of the ways in which the world is enchanted; and having taken my tour of duty in seminary instead of Vietnam, I think often about how these experiences shaped my current interests and work. I have been teaching the philosophy and methodology of interpretive work and doing fieldwork for several years now. One theme that runs through all that work is that I view the act of social inquiry as an emotional and moral undertaking and not simply, or even, an exercise of method.

I believe that in confronting the current controversies surrounding the nature and meaning of interpretive work—in worrying about notions of subjectivity and objectivity, whether to cultivate friendship or only rapport, whether to be empathetic or sympathetic, whether we can "represent" another's world, how our voice as author or scribe should be manifest in a text, and so forth—we are wrestling with problems of self-identity and relationship. These problems demand the union of intellect and passion; they require examination of the connections between self, other, and world, and reflection on what it is right to do and good to be as an inquirer.

Problems associated with this developing moral awareness of the act of inquiry do not wholly admit of solution; in fact, as T. S. Eliot once pointed out, they are altogether different than what we are accustomed to thinking of as methodological problems: They must be faced or lived rather than solved. They are examples of the moral demands of life and invoke the moral requirements of a practice—that is, they reflect and invoke the assumptions embedded in our methodological theories about such matters as the identity and authority of the inquirer; the responsibilities we have toward others; the aim and purpose of our work; the obligations to define and enact what we would traditionally call the classic virtues of temperance, courage, wisdom, and so forth.

I am often disheartened by the fact that we persist in arguing about the tools of our practice without asking just what our practice might be about. In the social sciences, we are extremely fond of learning, applying, and teaching techniques, methods, and procedures for how to *do* inquiry. The penchant is so great, in fact, that the feminist theologian Mary Daly (1973) has coined the term "methodolatry" to refer to the worship of method. While we are busying ourselves with acquiring methods expertise, we are paying too little attention to what it means to *be* an inquirer, or an educator, or an administrator, or a teacher for that matter. This is a practical (in an Aristotelian sense) and moral concern.

Serious reflection on the nature and purpose of interpretive inquiry raises questions of our being; it requires each of us to come to terms with a union of moral and cognitive concerns in our own and others' lived experience. Put somewhat differently, the question, "How shall I know these people I am studying?" is at once to answer the question, "How shall I *be* toward these people I am studying?" Much of my work, in methodology at least, continues to be preoccupied with answers to that question and their implications for the social practice of inquiry.

My Transition to Interpretive Inquiry

John K. Smith

When Lous and Keith asked me to write this story of how I came to qualitative research, I not only thought, but was bold enough to say, "No problem—I will dash off five or six pages for you in an afternoon over the semester break." Well, the semester break has come and gone; all I have to show for my efforts are various false starts, a number of very rough drafts that found their appropriate home in the wastebasket, and a draft that led Lous and Keith to pose various questions. A number of their questions made sense, and so I am at it once more. Recounting my shift from quantitative inquiry to interpretive inquiry has turned out to be much more difficult and confusing than I thought it ever could be.

I think I understand a good part of the reason for my difficulty and confusion. The problem is that I do not know rationally, at least as this term is commonly defined, why the shift occurred, yet I have been attempting to write this story as if I could give a more or less definitive account of what happened. But definitive answers are not available to these kinds of questions. I can present some possibilities, but they will always remain possibilities—and the possibilities of one day are not necessarily the possibilities of another day. None of this should come as a surprise to me. Intellectually, I have "known" for a long time that the reasons people do things are not only not transparent to others, they are not even transparent to the people themselves. After all, I have made this point in various articles over the years. It is rather ironic that when I come to write about myself I should have such trouble with one of the most basic insights of interpretive inquiry.

In my last draft I ended the above paragraph with the phrase "it is one thing to 'know' something, it is another thing to know something." I think I initially added this phrase less because I was convinced that it said anything interesting or important, but more because I thought it was a rather clever play on words. Now I realize that maybe I was being a little more insightful than I thought I was, because the phrase applies to my situation with this story. That is, I know how to write what I think about research, but I do not know nearly as well how to write why I have come to think about research the way I do. When my intellectually trained mind is allowed to dominate my writing, I may have some problems, but they are familiar, almost comfortable ones. When this is not the case, as it is now, I am unsure of what to do. In any event, if I could turn this into an intellectualized recounting of my past, I could write five or six pages and be done with it. But Lous and Keith won't let me do that—it is not possible this time to take the easy way out.

The general contours of my background can be recounted in a rather straightforward fashion. I had a somewhat unconventional doctoral program because of the nature of the Educational Policy Studies Department at the University of Wisconsin. The program allowed students to range widely over courses from different areas such as history, economics, sociology, and philosophy. Also, the program did not require very much work in the area of statistics/quantitative research methods. Certainly much less was required than is the case for, for example, a doctorate in educational psychology. So I had the basics in quantitative methods and then, more or less on my own, learned a number of things beyond the basics. I was well versed in the techniques of quantitative research, but never deeply socialized into that "technical" mode of thinking. But, that lack of deep socialization notwithstanding, there should be no mistake about my disposition upon leaving graduate school. I, like most people *trained* in educational research, thought that the term *research* meant, by definition, quantitative research.

When I took a position at the University of Northern Iowa, where I have remained for over 20 years, I was asked to teach an introductory educational research course. I do not recall particularly wanting to teach the course, but I did so and have continued to do so. (Although I must add that the content of the course is much different today than it was 20 years ago—much less on "how to" and much more on "why," or on conceptual or philosophical issues.) I also recall that I did a few research studies and undertook various evaluations of school programs—all, of course, of a quantitative nature.

For the first few years everything was going quite well for me—my class in research was well liked by students, my field evaluations were well thought of and brought in extra money, I published enough to get tenure, and so on. All the elements were in place for what I suspect many people would have said was the beginning of a reasonably decent career. Around 1977, however, I had come to the end of my interest in quantitative research and I stopped doing standard, quantitatively oriented research and field evaluations. For the next seven years I did not write or publish at all. Moreover, it even got to the point where I was only occasionally able to read quantitative studies.

Why did I stop doing research, virtually stop reading standard research studies, and eventually shift to an interpretive understanding of inquiry? Let me start from the negative side and say that I have a pretty good idea about was *not* the reason for this change. The reason was not an intellectual one and, for that matter, could not have been so because I did not really know much "intellectually" at that time. Certainly I did not know much about research. What I mean here is that although I knew how to apply the techniques of quantitative research, I had little notion of why I was applying those techniques other than that I thought, vaguely so, that it had something to do with the search for truth.

I might also add that while I had read with interest some interpretive-type studies, such as those by Waller (1932), Jackson (1968), and Rist (1973), and was acquainted with some methods texts on ethnography, I had no more of a serious understanding of this perspective than I did of the quantitative one. Although I do not remember exactly my understanding of qualitative inquiry, I suspect that I saw it as not much more than an alternative, and I guess complementary, set of research techniques.

If the intellect is not the main factor in this story, then what is? As I said, I do not really know. What I do remember, however, was an almost physical reaction of avoidance to quantitative research that increased gradually in me over the course of the early to mid-1970s. For example, I definitely remember the time I was writing up an evaluation a number of us had done of an innovative program. During the writeup a number of things that had been building up in me came to the front: "I cannot stand this anymore . . . This questionnaire/statistical analysis stuff is driving me crazy. . . . None of it makes any sense anyway. . . . What is this, research/evaluation as a board game? . . . this is going to be my last evaluation" (it was).

Also, I can remember clearly how I was engaged in struggle between a feeling of obligation to read professional things (i.e., standard research articles) and a strong desire to read other things, such as history, philosophy, the few qualitative/ethnographic studies that were available, and especially novels. For a while this obligation/desire split led me to split my day, and myself for that matter, into two parts. During the day—my professional part—I would allow only professional reading and discussions. However, after that, the evenings were for "other things." It was at this time that I began to stop taking work home with me—or, rather,

I would take my briefcase home with work in it, but rarely opened it. Over time, however, the "other things" gradually, but inexorably, began to win out and invade the "professional things." The more I read, for example, the novels of García Marquez and the histories of Tuchman, the less I was able to read research on time-on-task, and so on.

It was in late 1979/early 1980 that someone suggested that I read Rorty's (1979) *Philosophy and the Mirror of Nature.* I am sure there are other events that made a significant difference in my thinking, but this one stands out at the moment. The first time I read this book I had only a shaky understanding intellectually of what he was talking about. But, that notwithstanding, somehow what he was saying made sense to me, and I was taken with his arguments. Obviously, I do not mean "made sense" in an analytical way, nor do I mean "taken" in an intellectual sense. This would not have been possible because, although I had been reading a fair amount of philosophy up to that time, I had not read nearly enough, especially philosophy of science, to engage his arguments at a scholarly level. It was just that what he was saying simply "felt right" to me—"right" enough, I might add, to completely put to rest my day/evening—professional/other split. Since then, I generally have read whatever I feel like whenever I feel like it, and what I feel like rarely includes quantitative research. I guess I feel about reading the latter much like I feel about reading, for example, my insurance policies—I guess it is something I should do, and maybe I will get around to it some day.

As I write this I also wonder if it was not fortunate that I did know so little philosophy of science when I read Rorty. What would have happened if I had read him differently, more philosophically (as many have) and less rhetorically, or even literarily? My wonder here is not a call to let ignorance be our guide; it is only to acknowledge the well-known point that knowledge is much more than "formal" knowledge, that is, knowledge of the head, and that formal knowledge alone can entrap as easily as it can liberate. Either way, I do not know what would have happened and, of course, there is no way to know.

From Rorty it was only a short step to a whole lot of other people—Bernstein (1983), Putnam (1981), Gadamer (1975), Giddens (1976), and so on. The tangible result was that three years later I published my first article on qualitative inquiry, one that has been followed by many other pieces, including two books (Smith, 1989, 1993).

I have read over this story and must add one more comment. I have attributed my difficulty with telling this story, rather than simply intellectualizing it, to my training. I likewise have attributed to my training my early concerns about not mixing my professional life and personal life. Maybe there is another reason. Is it possible that my unease and concern have something to do with the fact that I am male? I wonder if my female colleagues have felt as much unease and have had as much difficulty with their stories. I am beginning to doubt it—it is time that I ask them.

3

Wishing the Future

I know that there is nothing absolute or objectively valid, that knowledge must seep into your blood, into your self, not just into your head, that you must live it. And here I always come back to what one should strive after with all one's might: one must marry one's feelings to one's beliefs and ideas. That is probably the only way to achieve a measure of harmony in one's life.

Etty Hillesum (1983, p. 48)

It is necessary to remember that it is first the potential oppressor within that we must resist—the potential victim within that we must rescue—otherwise we cannot hope for an end to domination, for liberation . . .

bell hooks (1989, p. 21)

Beyond "Eureka":
The Pursuit of
Transformative Inquiry

JAMES P. ANGLIN

I put off writing my earlier "Eureka! Bathed in Transformation" to the last possible moment. My procrastination resulted from two fears: one that I would not be able to write the story, and the other that I would indeed write it, thereby exposing my vulnerabilities for all to see. I believe that there was also a somatic dimension to the delay. This combination of personal and scholarly writing is something I do best with my body in one place for a short, concentrated period of time, and, when written this way, my writing is less liable to overcensoring by my critical, analytic mode. Once again, I have been avoiding writing this piece also, not even responding to the prompting faxes from the editors. The last fax had only one word on it—URGENT! So it is now or never.

My first publication following the "Eureka" experience was a chapter in a book on ecological research methods in which I tentatively put forward my experience in print, buried in the middle of some more traditional analysis of the literature and relevant issues (Anglin, 1988). But my phenomenological/interpretive perspective was not missed by the author of the preface, whose work had greatly informed all of the contributors to the book—Urie Bronfenbrenner. He spent a significant portion of his preface trying to distance himself from my analysis of the strong phenomenological orientation evident (to me) in his now classic work *The Ecology of Human Development* (1979). I did not draft a rebuttal to his preface, nor did I correspond with him, as I did not feel ready to argue methodology with such a giant in the field of psychological research.

As I noted at the end of my earlier chapter, my shifting orientation to research led me to spend much of a study leave attempting to mine a number of veins of qualitative, phenomenological, and interpretive theory and research methods, crossing the disciplines of sociology, education, psychology, anthropology, the physical sciences, and philosophy. I continued to be involved in occasional seminars and conference sessions focusing on innovative research methods, and I found myself being asked to sit on committees and to serve as the external examiner for students undertaking interpretive theses within the university. One professor on the education faculty was particularly successful in attracting students into her classes on interpretive inquiry and hermeneutics, and a series of fascinating studies, several of which pushed my understanding and methodological openmindedness to their limits, helped me to keep thinking and reflecting about methods and directions for future research.

Several of my convictions concerning the nature and role of the researcher were reinforced or clarified over this period of graduate committee work. First, the notion of the researcher as the prime research instrument in the social sciences (in all sciences?) was further strengthened as I witnessed more people (students and faculty) engaged in this work. Second, the critical importance of conceptual clarity and writing skills (preferably including creative writing skills) to the task of interpretive research was demonstrated repeatedly. Third, the need for the researcher to be consciously engaged in a personal quest into unknown territory of self also became apparent. I have experienced a number of students and faculty struggling to transform themselves in order to understand aspects of self, the world, and other people more fully, more richly, and more deeply. There seemed to be few (if any) road maps available to them, and they always seemed to be caught up in an almost epic journey characterized by an often tortured interweaving of excitement, despair, joy, agony, compulsion, liberation, fear, attraction, doubt, and conviction. Usually they produced writing that was personally meaningful, insightful, and informative about a phenomenon or phenomena, but that was extremely challenging and provocative for the reader (at least this one).

Once, as an external examiner, I postponed an oral defense because, even given what I consider to be an open and tolerant orientation on my part, I wasn't sure if the student had "lost it." After an hour-and-a-half dialogue with her in the presence of her committee, I concluded that what she was doing was legitimate, and that she knew well enough what she was doing and (perhaps more importantly) what she was not doing. This experience clarified for me the importance of a researcher being able to situate one's inquiry and approach within the evolving tradition of scholarly work. This student and her committee were challenging the traditional criteria for what distinguished a thesis from a story, description from analysis, poetry from prose, self from other, and scholarly work from lived experience. In the process, they were severely challenging my understandings as well. The experience highlighted the risks that faculty members and students take when they push the limits of convention, in topic, content, and format, and it demonstrated the degree of interpretation involved in trying to "uphold the standards of the University" for graduate work. As the external examiner, it was my responsibility to ensure that largely undefined standards were being adhered to, but given the lack of specificity (which I do not suggest changing), I realized that the experimental nature of the method forced me to create a new interpretation of the parameters of my own understanding, and to reflect quite actively on the judgments I was required to make to play the role of "representative of the University." I could not simply respond as an individual reader and researcher on the basis of my personal preferences alone. What I was being asked to do was to uphold the integrity of the evolving scholarly enterprise as I understood it.

All through this time, I have been trying to enhance my understanding of the modes of human knowing and the processes characterizing personal, organizational, and societal learning. This process has included the opportunity to work with groups of 12 to 18 graduate students in seminars on "promoting professional and community learning" and "advanced program design." I have found that with each subsequent opportunity, I have been expanding my beliefs and understandings regarding teaching and learning and pushing these understandings up to and beyond their limits. That is, I am now more often setting off in a direction without worrying so much about not being clear about the ultimate destination. I am learning that there are few readily available maps for where I, and the students, need and want to go. Therefore, we are learning to be satisfied with having a compass, usually a set of shared values, beliefs, and learning objectives, which we articulate together early in the process (course) and which we have faith will guide us to new and important (at least for us) territories of learning. So far, the journeys have been more rewarding than frustrating for most of us, most of the time, but such learning seems to necessitate a certain amount of personal pain and collective struggle.

Congruence, between what is being studied and how it is being studied, between what the instructor espouses and how the instructor behaves, between what is being learned and how it is being assessed, and between how we (students and instructors) talk about relationships and how we relate to each other, has become increasingly important and explicit as a class objective in itself. That is, process objectives have evolved to be as important, and on occasion more important, than content objectives. The biggest surprise (and pleasure) for me has been to experience how much more content is learned (not just covered) when careful and concentrated attention is paid to the group learning environment and process, encompassing both students and instructors in their interactive and mutual learning and teaching.

What does this have to do with interpretive research and methods? I think that both research and teaching are means for engaging ourselves, the world, and each other in an attempt to create deeper mutual understanding throughout society. I believe that participants in both enterprises need to be engaged as full persons, with all of their faculties being acknowledged in a spirit of mutual exploration.

The spiritual aspect has been the latest dimension to capture my attention. We talk quite offhandedly about "the spirit of inquiry," "inspiring teachers," "school spirit," and so on. Reading the work of Harrison Owen (1987, 1990, 1991), an organizational consultant and priest, has helped to focus my own thinking and experiencing in the area of spirit, and has encouraged me to begin talking about the nature and significance of spirit in organizations—businesses, human services, schools, universities, and governments—with those who show some receptivity to the topic. Owen (1987) uses the word *transformation* to indicate change that is not just "more and faster," but different in "kind and quality." I am using the term "transformative inquiry" to refer to an approach to engaging the world and other persons that is not just more of the same, but of a different kind and quality. I have come to see that the "Eureka"–type experience I have written about earlier is not a one-time change. Rather, it is the first transformative change in a series of changes that will occur if one continues to push up to and beyond the limits of one's understanding on an ongoing basis.

The concept of transformation is certainly not a novel one. Adult learning theorists (e.g., Mezirow, 1990) have been exploring the concept for some time, and a great many recent books and articles have been written about "transforming government," "transforming the university," "transforming the family," and transforming just about any other human organization you can imagine.

What is new is a reclaiming of the role of spirit in this process. While some writers have been circling around it, and perhaps hinting at it for some time, it is only recently that academics have begun to admit the concept of spirit into their writing and theorizing. One of these is Harvard University child psychiatrist Robert Coles, whose book *The Spiritual Life of Children* (1990) has helped to reintroduce and make acceptable (if not yet fully respectable) academic study of the spiritual dimension of persons and society. Ironically, from their inception and for centuries thereafter, universities in Western Europe were dominated by conceptions of the religious and spiritual, right up to relatively recent times. Modern conceptions of research arose within the paradigm of the scientific method, which began to displace religion from its preeminent position in academia in the 17th and 18th centuries.

It is telling to note how Coles came to address the subject of the spiritual life of children. In 1978, when Coles was well published and well advanced in his career, Anna Freud made a suggestion to him: "It would be of interest if you went over your earlier work and looked for what you might have missed back then" (Coles, 1990, p. xiii). Coles remembers being somewhat amused and perplexed by this suggestion, and it wasn't until seven or eight years later that he decided to follow her advice. The resulting project on the spiritual life of children took many years to complete, and, in Coles's own words, it "finally helped me see children as seekers, as young pilgrims well aware that life is a finite journey and as anxious to make sense of it as those of us who are farther along in the time allotted us" (Coles, 1990, p. xvi).

To my mind, the recent surge of interest in interpretive inquiry evident in the social science literature and in portions of academia may be related to a resurgence of the deep need to explore, in a concerted and serious way, the personal and social meaning of this "finite journey." Traditional scientific research approaches had defined this quest as residing outside its "rigorous and verifiable" (or at least, "falsifiable" [Popper, 1986]) domain.

Whatever the reason for its emergence at this time, there appears to be a current need and opportunity within the scholarly domain to explore the spiritual dimension of our life and work. It is a research that is fraught with difficulties, complexities, and confusion. If spirit is intangible, how does one study it? I do not pretend to have the answer. What is perhaps most important at this juncture is simply recognizing this domain as an important area for inquiry.

Sam Keen (1990) has a definition of teaching that has applicability, I believe, to the human science research enterprise and the manner in which people are prepared to undertake such work. Keen says, "The chief function of the teacher is to give students permission to allow exiled portions of their own personalities to return home and be welcomed" (p. 68). It may be that one of the most significant recent developments that will have an important impact on the research enterprise (in all of its manifestations) over the coming decades will be the acknowledgment of the lost spiritual parts of ourselves, and their need to be welcomed home to our projects of individual and collective inquiry and development.

While I am far from sure what all of this will mean in practice, it seems clear that it will serve to heighten the critical role of the researcher in the research enterprise, and that it will entail much more attention being paid to the quality of being and self-development of the student/ researcher as a person, as well as to the role of faculty members as mentors and guides.

Much attention has been given in recent years to ways of knowing and learning styles (see, for example, Belenky, Clinchy, Goldberger, & Tarule, 1986; Myers, 1980). However, this literature has been primarily grounded in, extrapolations from, and modest critiques of traditional psychological research. Recently, Margaret Donaldson (1992) has been probing the development of human minds, beginning with the most recent psychological research findings on infants and children, and moving into quite speculative but intriguing exploration of historical and religious experience as they relate to spiritual development. Her persuasive (to me) analysis suggests that there are "modes of the mind" of an emotional (in its broadest sense) kind that parallel the advanced cognitive modes but that are not well conceptualized nor documented in the more traditional academic literature. Basically, she posits two types and two levels of knowing of an advanced nature. The two cognitive modes are well known and acknowledged, which she terms "intellectual construct" and "intellectual transcendent." What is most challenging is Donaldson's postulating of two additional modes in the emotional sphere. She refers to these as "value-sensing modes," existing at the construct and transcendent levels paralleling the two advanced intellectual modes. In brief, the "value-sensing construct mode [is] one in which there is an apprehension of transpersonal importance, powerfully felt, but where the functioning of the mode [depends] upon the support of the imagination" (p. 150). In other words, the imagination is necessary to provide the imaginary context built up from the everyday experiences of things, people, and events in the world. Further, explanation of these events, persons, and things is the main aim of this mode.

The major difference in the value-sensing transcendent mode from the value-sensing construct mode is that the need for a constructed context is not there. That is, self-transcending values are, in this mode, experienced and responded to without recourse to "the props" provided by the working of the imagination (p. 151). Donaldson observes that these two modes, and especially the transcendent one, are less familiar to us than their intellectual or cognitive counterparts. She suggests that this may be because the emotional response is more difficult to systematically record and to codify. Donaldson further suggests that the two value-sensing "modes of mind" may represent "two modes of apprehending the divine" (spirit), which are emotional and experiential rather than intellectual (p. 156). Without attempting to present Donaldson's work any further, I simply wish to indicate that there do exist attempts by contemporary researchers and academics in the West to explore and understand the basis for our spiritual development as human beings, acknowledging that within some other cultures spiritual development is central to knowledge and to life.

In other words, following Donaldson, we can no longer focus so exclusively on "dispassionate" modes of inquiry, and on traditional cognitive ways of knowing. Donaldson is pointing in the direction of a more integrated understanding of human development, in which psychology too holds that the emotional, moral, and spiritual dimensions of human beings can be fostered and cared for more fully than heretofore has been believed. It has long been observed that the intellectual, rational, and technical dimensions of human beings have developed far beyond our emotional, moral, and spiritual capacities, and an approach to research that offers the potential of addressing this imbalance needs to be taken seriously indeed.

In summary, I am suggesting that interpretive inquiry can lead to what I have termed "transformative inquiry," and that what characterizes the transformative enterprise is an understanding that spirit and spiritual development are at the heart of personal, scholarly, and organizational life and, therefore, of change. The work of such people as Margaret Donaldson, Harrison Owen, and Robert Coles has contributed to my understanding and sense of direction, and may offer guidance for broader work in the field of human inquiry in the decades ahead.

Finding the Ghost in the Machine and Giving It Back Its Body

KEITH BALLARD

I am writing this in December, which is the beginning of summer here in New Zealand. For many there is the anticipation of a holiday and a change to the rhythm of our lives for a while, with perhaps some new experiences, new thoughts, new plans. It is a time to reflect on who you are near the end of another year.

The summer vacation is when I catch up on novels set aside in the face of other demands over the preceding months. I used to think that such reading should only be fitted in outside of work times (how I admire John Smith's decision to read just what he chose—what a marvelously subversive idea). But in recent years I have acknowledged that too long without a story and I feel unsettled, isolated, deprived of something important that helps locate me beyond my immediate self and circumstances. So, while the holiday season remains a special indulgence, I no longer resist the fiction shelves at other times. I recently finished Michael Ondaatje's (1992) *The English Patient*, and I still have the feeling that I was with those people in that decaying villa outside Florence, struggling with the moral dilemmas of their lives. It is a curious and marvelous experience, losing yourself, dissolving into another place and time, and I feel that this is knowing with the real me, mind, body, and soul.

I think that this may be a similar kind of knowing to that described by James Anglin in his account of insights in the bath. As I read his story I immediately recognized the perceptual and sensory events that accompanied the transformation of his ideas and the reconceptualization of his worldview, and recalled an experience of my own from many years ago. I had been trying to understand Donne, Ibsen, Beckett, and other writers assigned in my undergraduate English literature course, and remember focusing intensely on this work, really wanting to know what it all meant. On this particular day, from something I was reading, I saw that there was a key to this puzzle—it had to do with conceits and metaphors, as I recall. The revelation expressed itself in an overwhelming sensation, much like James's in his bathtub, of delight, excitement, physical energy, many intellectual realizations flowing one from another, all inextricably merged with the sun pouring through the window, the harbor below, turquoise and brilliant, a huge Don Binney bird painting on the wall across the room from me, everything seeming to "make sense," experienced in a sensual and emotional way, yet with an analytical clarity that I think I rarely achieve. I am sure that the intellectual understandings I came to that day, while new to me, were really quite ordinary, but the sensory experience was extraordinary. I am indebted to James Anglin for affirming a kind of experience that has always seemed to me to have importance, but that I have not previously come across in professional discourse (although for a remarkably similar fictional account, see Alther, 1990, pp. 433–434).

I have found it difficult to write about myself for this book, feeling anxious about how the exposed "I" will be judged by others. But it is something that I think I owe all of those research "subjects" whose responses and experiences I have laid out on the pages of books and journals over the years. It seemed time to talk about who was trying to tell their stories, and why.

Other researchers who have already located themselves in their work have provided a context for identifying, in Evelyn Fox Keller's (1985) terms, research as a "deeply personal" activity (p. 7), reflecting our "prior emotional commitments, expectations, and desires" (p. 10). The stories in Chapter 2 of this book show researchers as real, live, thinking and feeling people, with uncertainties and vulnerabilities, and I was delighted to get to know something about them. I felt connected with them in a way that I rarely do when reading research literature.

Humans are curious about one another. Our fascination, whether with a Shakespearean play or with a TV soap or sitcom, reflects a desire to know about other people's experiences, decisions, motives, joy, and pain. This is how we learn about ourselves. By observing or by vicariously trying out an experience or a role, we expand our notion of who we might be, both in terms of who is like us, as we conceive and construct and reconstruct ourselves, and who is not like us. This is one of the ways in which we learn how we should be toward and with others, especially those who we may see as different from ourselves in terms of gender, culture, or other ways. As Ben Okri (1993) writes in *Songs of Enchantment*, "Stories can conquer fear, you know. They can make the heart bigger" (p. 46).

How do they do that? How is it that a while back I found Nadine

Gordimer's (1990) *My Son's Story* in parts so powerful, so painful, so overwhelming, that I could sometimes read only a few pages at a time? How is it that I can feel that I have met Mary Poplin (when I have not) and have visited classrooms with her? Somehow both of these people are a part of what is driving my current research. This is not in terms of particular concepts or systems of ideas — I would be hard pressed to offer an intellectual analysis of the stories that I refer to here. Somehow the experiences they describe have made sense to me; they have become part of how I attend to the world. "Sense" really is the right word here; it is my body, my embodied self, that is at ease within this experience. For the future, we need to create research that achieves such a communion.

I think that story will be important in this regard. Jean Clandinin and Michael Connelly (1991) describe *story* as a "basic phenomenon of life" and a "fundamental method of personal (and social) growth" (p. 259). Robert Donmoyer (1990) proposes that the value of stories, narratives, and case studies is that they make complex issues meaningful in a way that individuals can use. Narratives, suggests Donmoyer, provide "vicarious experience . . . [and] create a virtual reality, that is, a reality that exists within our imaginations" (p. 192). In this way, says Donmoyer, such accounts become part of an individual's own experience, and so can be adapted and applied, in all their complexity, to other settings and other people. I suggest that Donmoyer has it right. Stories, not any bizarre computerized process, create virtual reality. While we may allow computers to engage with our minds and trick our perceptions, only stories can be truly "tools of enchantment" (Witherell & Noddings, 1991, p. 279): magical experiences that can involve our whole selves and touch our soul, but which, nevertheless, can be exposed to critical reflection in terms of their contribution to our understandings of theory and practice, values and ethics (Goodman, 1992), and their "competitive resistance" to alternative, plausible accounts (Schön, 1991, p. 348).

I found the stories in Chapter 2 to be affirming and empowering. This comes from knowing that others see uncertainty and complexity as central to their research experience, to be enjoyed and worked with, rather than to be fought against or managed by research methodology. The writing of previously hidden experiences is a way of supporting discussion about embodied knowing in research. It is also a way of linking researchers with one another, of building bridges between researchers and other writers and artists who are exploring who we are and what we are about, and of sharing ideas on how we might undertake research from a basis of values, our sense of morality, and our sense of our changing selves.

In order to achieve that, I think we will need to work in the kind of ways that we have tried here. That is, to consciously and openly include ourselves in our work and writing about that work, and to research ourselves as creators and constructors of research. In the past we have exposed the data and interpretations of our research to scrutiny. We have critiqued the research method as if that were the foundation of the work. It is now time to look at the ghost in these research machines, that is, at ourselves. This means focusing on research as an essentially human activity and as therefore embedded in personal, social, cultural, political, historical, spiritual, and gendered bodies and contexts. What has the researcher not seen or sensed or said? What different interpretations might emerge from the emotions and realities of others? Such complexity, the acknowledgment of contradictions, of alternative meanings and explanations, and of somatic experiences, would make research an exciting and humanizing enterprise.

Our turn to interpretive research and to other, more participatory strategies was driven by our need for personal contact with those we wanted to understand — as Lous Heshusius expressed it, a need for experience of "real people, real lives, real knowledge." Opening up to people in this way exposes our motives to their scrutiny. Who will benefit from this work? Can the researcher be trusted to "get it right," especially when he or she may be different in background and experience from those whose lives are the focus of a study? Is there still a "getting it right"? Once we stop thinking of ourselves as objective arbiters of truth, these things really matter and are at the core of what we do.

I have struggled with these issues as a participant in action research and research as personal narrative, the telling of stories. Involvement in this work, in particular trying to support empowerment and democratic dialogue for everyone taking part, was marvelously and sometimes, in the case of the action research study, impossibly complex. This is not comfortable research. At a basic level, it comes down to, "Will these people like me (and why or why not)?" What I want to reflect on briefly here are some aspects of my experience as a researcher in such studies. The challenge has involved the moral issue raised earlier in this volume by Thomas Schwandt, who asked, "How shall I *be* toward these people I am studying?"

The action research project ran across four years, and involved 143 families of children who have disabilities and 74 professionals working in health, education, and welfare agencies (Ballard, Watson, Bray, Burrows, & MacArthur, 1992). It was parent-driven, and came to focus around information, support, advocacy, networking, and parents contributing to professional training programs. From our own and from independent reports, the project impacted on policy and practice in education, health, and welfare at a local and, to some extent, national level. So it achieved the goal of action research, which is to develop a group of people who support one another in a critical analysis of their situation so that all participants may use those understandings, individually and collectively, in action for change. The demands on time were considerable. The openly ideological nature of the work gave the researchers a political profile in academic and public arenas such that criticism was often an attack on one's motives and values—much harder to deal with than the usual politics of research method. What was, and remains, sustaining is the shared learning that comes from direct contact with parents and caregivers whose unremitting energy and love (and exhaustion, pain, and marginalization) may not otherwise be known by an outsider.

This is the point that I want to stress here. In the disability area, mine is not an authentic voice—I am not disabled, nor are my children. So what role do I have? Clearly I should not speak for or about people whose experiences I do not share. Researchers have been accused by feminists (Westkott, 1979) and by minority groups (Oliver, 1992) of misunderstanding and misinterpreting realities of which the researcher is not a part.

Yet on issues of oppression and disempowerment, researchers, as part of their community, may be seen as either part of the solution or part of the problem. In New Zealand, for example, Ranginui Walker (1990) has said that it is not for Maori alone to solve the problems that they now experience as a result of 150 years of colonization. He says that Pakeha (European) New Zealanders "are as much a part of social transformation in the post-colonial era as radical and activist Maori" (p. 234). In England, Mike Oliver (1992) has made a similar point about disability, saying that the focus of research needs to move from disabled people and on to disabilist society. The majority who are not disabled are inevitably a part of disability issues in their society, and need to address the roles they play in creating, or in challenging, disabling theories and practices.

Such a breaking down of the distance between people is discussed by Mike Oliver (1992) in his case for "changing the social relations of research production" (p. 101), a theme that seems close to Thomas Schwandt's concern for how we should be toward others. Oliver works from the position that disability is created by social arrangements that both fail to support and are actively oppressive of people who experience sensory, physical, or other impairments. He sees research as part of these social arrangements. Research has largely been undertaken by people who lack direct experience of disability, says Oliver. It has benefited the researchers while failing to challenge the inadequacies of "social engineering" (positivist) and "social enlightenment" (interpretive) research, which has had little, if any, impact on the sociopolitical construction of disability. Oliver suggests that what is needed is an emancipatory paradigm. This would focus on disabilist societies, rather than disabled people, and researchers (disabled or otherwise) would be accountable to, and work toward empowerment with, people experiencing disability. In such approaches, says Oliver, "both researcher and researched become changers and changed" (p. 107).

In the Family Network project (Ballard et al., 1992), we tried to reduce the gap between research and action, and researcher and other participants, by working as a group for commonly agreed-upon goals. It was not easy, and our goals were not always achieved. A feature of such work—and sometimes a source of stress, misunderstanding, emotion, and struggle—is its complexity, diversity, and intensely personal nature. When things get really messy, and they do, the researcher must take care not to be in control, not to "make sense" of what is happening. As Mary Poplin suggests in her story in Chapter 2 of this book, it is the insiders that need to name the problem. It is also the case that those in minority, subordinate positions typically know their own as well as the perspective of powerful others, and so they may already have a more complex, multifaceted view of the world than many researchers (hooks, 1990; Nielsen, 1990). If, as researchers, we stopped deliberately or inadvertently assimilating and colonizing the worldview of others (for example, by our coded language and conventions of writing style), then we might be able to recognize and value multiple realities and what they can teach us.

It is not just in the social sciences that such a respect for difference is being urged. Evelyn Fox Keller (1985) writes of Nobel prize–winning geneticist Barbara McClintock's work that she valued difference for what it can tell us, and notes that

> Making difference understandable does not mean making it disappear
> . . . respect for difference remains content with multiplicity as an end
> in itself . . . [and] provides a starting point for relatedness. (p. 163)

In situations where "they," by virtue of gender, ethnicity, sexual orientation, power, or experience, are different, how does the researcher relate to others whose lives we are not an immediate part of? What might engage our "capacity for empathy" (Keller, 1985, p. 164)? I think that the virtual reality of stories, narratives, biographies, and other personal accounts has a significant role in this regard. Critics suggest that such an approach fails to deal with issues of false consciousness (Carr & Kem-

mis, 1986), treats minority issues as if they were simply misunderstand-
ings that could be solved by "enlightenment," and fails to directly confront oppressive acts and structures (Atkin, 1991; Oliver, 1992). I do
not agree that this is the whole picture. Unquestionably we may feel
morally bound as researchers (and citizens) to join with others and act
directly on social and educational problems. But stories can help us
understand the nature of these problems, and to see why they are important. Stories can be a way for different participants to describe, analyze,
and explain their experiences in their own way. This in itself may be
empowering for those who have not often been heard in the development
of policy and practice. bell hooks (1989), for example, suggests that
women of color, as well as other minority groups, must theorize and
advance their cause in their own voice if they are to overcome their
domination. Stories can be one way to achieve this and to resist the
"elitism in . . . work that is linguistically convoluted" (hooks, 1989, p.
36). The power of stories is that they can communicate complex experiences, emotions, and ideas in a way that is commonly accessible.

I recently worked with some self-advocates (adults who have intellectual disabilities), parents and *whanau* (extended family) of children
who have disabilities, and Maori and Pakeha researchers (Ballard,
1994). Our goal was to write personal accounts of the lived experience
of disability in New Zealand communities (my own story was about
being a researcher in this area). We thought that this might lead to
understanding and action on policy and practice in the disability area.
Time will tell. But I think that many readers may recognize something of
themselves in the human experiences of grief, joy, passion, oppression,
liberation, exclusion, valuing, caring, inclusion, injustice, struggle, cele-
bration, and achievement that these various accounts describe as taking
place in our communities.

In our action research study (Ballard et al., 1992), we found evidence that nondisabled people who spent time with disabled children
and their families gained in understanding and in support for inclusive
policies and practice. I think that stories of disability may act in a similar
way for those that cannot "be there." Clearly action, changes in personal
behavior and direct challenges to disabilist individuals and institutions,
not just empathy and enlightenment, is required. But I think that research as stories can be part of the complex web of experiences that will
help us to understand and value our differences, our common humanity,
and our interdependencies. That must be a good basis, if not an impetus,
for action.

Our stories of disability are by Maori and Pakeha. In New Zealand,
many of the indigenous Maori people support the idea that we are a
bicultural nation, reflecting the Treaty of 1840 between Maori and the

English crown on which our present society was founded. We are also now a multicultural nation, but the idea of biculturalism is that the contract by which Europeans (Pakeha) negotiated with Maori the right to be here requires that first, in thought and action, we must honor the cultural perspective of both Maori and Pakeha. From that position we relate to the other cultures that make up our community.

Biculturalism is an attempt to redress the hegemonic dominance exerted by Western European thought in this country, by working within two worldviews. In particular, it requires sharing in power and decision-making. For me, a particularly striking aspect of Maori culture is the emphasis given to sustaining and supportive relationships between people, in contrast to the more individualistic perspective of my own European experience. For Maori, communication, responsibility, and accountability reflect group processes, which in turn reflect issues of involvement and interdependence (Bishop & Glynn, 1992). The Maori individual is inextricably linked with others and with the natural and spiritual world. This is acknowledged in procedures that are a part of everyday life. So, for example, in two research groups in which I am presently a participant, our meetings begin and close with a karakia (*prayer*) that relates us to the spiritual world, to the thoughts of others and to the environment that sustains us. I am not a conventionally religious person, but such experiences have begun to reaffirm my spirituality. They center me in who I am, and relate me to place, purpose, and people. All things, say Maori, have a *mauri*, a life essence. A book or a building may be so imbued (Barlow, 1991). Such a thought engenders respect and relatedness.

This is now a part of my journey toward the reenchantment of my worldview. While stressing the importance of involvement with others, feminist art historian Suzie Gablik (1991) suggests that the way to "prepare the ground" for new ways of understanding the world is to "make changes in one's own life" (p. 8).

Reading the stories in Chapter 2 of this book helped confirm for me that there is a "hidden history" (Berman, 1989) of embodied knowing in our lives and therefore in our research. It is time to reclaim and identify with these experiences. They will help us refeel and rethink the relationships involved in research and in other aspects of our lives. The stories of our various developmental experiences presented here show that to do so means, in Suzie Gablik's words, "stepping beyond the modern traditions of mechanism, positivism, empiricism, rationalism, materialism, secularism and scientism — the whole objectifying consciousness of the Enlightenment — in a way that allows for a return of soul" (p. 11). Then we may see in all things an essence of which we are a part.

Acknowledging the Why of Method

Curt Dudley-Marling

It's interesting how many of the contributors to this volume acknowledged the attraction reductive methodologies held for them early in their careers. Keith Ballard, for example, found applied behavior analysis attractive at one point because of its "explanatory elegance." Mary Poplin found that "conjugat[ing] . . . millions of academic tasks into small behavioral objectives" resonated well with her "desire for order and control." The attraction quantitative research held for John Smith may be more typical. He, like most people trained in educational research, thought that the term research meant, by definition, quantitative research.

It is widely assumed that quantitative research is what scientists do. Therefore, rejecting THE scientific method risks being seen as "not a real scientist" or, worse, not having one's work taken seriously. Witness Egon Guba's being "almost laughed off the podium" for his "unscientific proposals." I remember being stung several years ago by the criticism from a prominent researcher that qualitative researchers were "soft-headed." I also recall participating in a forum where a well-known psychologist dismissed out of hand the opinions of an outstanding teacher, author, and teacher-researcher because she had no (quantitative) data to support her views. Earlier in the day he had challenged this teacher to back up her statements "with the data." By the end of the day he literally turned his back on her whenever she spoke. Having nothing he considered "real data," she was, apparently, not even worth listening to.

In this part of my paper I'd like to consider the attraction of reductive methods within the context of what John Dewey (1960) referred to as the "Quest for Certainty." Then I'll take up a theme introduced by Thomas Schwandt: research as a moral enterprise.

Occam's Razor: The Quest for Certainty

In *Voltaire's Bastards*, John Ralston Saul (1992) observes that "our un-quenchable thirst for answers has become one of the obvious characteris-tics of the West in the second half of the twentieth century" (p. 16). Ours isn't the first age, however, that has sought to explain the world we inhabit. Explaining and predicting events in the physical world has al-ways been vital for our survival. Predicting animal migration patterns and the coming of the seasons, for example, helped ancient peoples determine the best times for hunting and planting crops. A failure to understand the physical world could easily have led *homo sapiens* to early extinction. Regrettably, our mastery of the world has hastened the extinction of many other species and may, eventually, risk our own.

What sets us apart from previous epochs, it seems to me, is the conceit that we can know everything with complete certainty. Earlier generations of people were probably no less sure of what they knew, but they were more likely to allow that significant dimensions of their universe—specifically, that spiritual world inhabited by souls and dei-ties—were unknowable. Men and women could at best only guess at God's grand design, even if they accepted that certain received texts—usually interpreted by others—revealed God's plan for how they should lead their lives. In the second half of the 20th century, it is the conven-tional wisdom that everything in our universe is knowable and that we can (and shall) know (be able to explain/predict) it. This hubris stems from the conviction that we have discovered the ultimate tool for know-ing: reason.

Reason did succeed in liberating European peasants from the tyr-anny of received (religious) knowledge that oppressed them in the centu-ries before the Enlightenment (Saul, 1992). Rational knowing imposes its own tyranny, however. Valorizing reason as the ultimate means of knowing leads us to fail to take seriously points of view of individuals who are dismissed as "irrational," "unscientific," or "superstitious." I imagine this is how Guba got into trouble with some of his colleagues. More seriously, the presumption that certain views are irrational (read: not rational) allows us to marginalize the views of entire groups. I'll say more about this later.

The tyranny of reason also has the effect of fixing our attention on that part of our physical and social world that is "knowable" to reason to the exclusion of other (significant) sectors of reality. Reason compels us to embark on a quest for certainty that "can be fulfilled in pure knowing alone" (Dewey, 1960, p. 8). John Dewey (1960) is describing the rational person when he observes that:

> Perfect certainty is what man [sic] wants. It cannot be found by practi-
> cal doing or making; these take effect in an uncertain future, and
> involve peril, the risk of misadventure, frustration and failure. Knowl-
> edge, on the other hand, is thought to be concerned with a region of
> being which is fixed in itself. (p. 21)

Herein lies the attraction of quantitative research, applied behavior analysis, and other reductive methods. Constructing the "perfect certainty . . . man wants" requires that the world be reduced to tiny bits (here I imagine a bumper sticker: "REAL SCIENTISTS DO IT IN BITS") removed from the uncertain world of practical activity. This quest for certainty accounts for the privileging of knowing over doing (as if these are separable), which, in the world of education, relegates teachers as doers to the role of (mere) workers carrying out the designs of researchers who are the knowers. Per-haps this accounts for my "well-known psychologist's" irritation with the teacher. By presuming to "know," she threatened his privilege as one who knows, that is, one who produces knowledge.

The problem here is obvious, but our rational tendencies prevent many people from seeing it: a world we know with "complete certainty" fulfilled in "pure knowing" and separate from practical activity is an abstraction. It takes human beings to a place of perfect knowing and perfect certainty, a place previously reserved for gods. This is a place we can imagine, but it is not a place where we actually live. The messy reality we inhabit bears only the faintest resemblance to the socially constructed reality of pure knowing. The place where real people live their mundane lives is fraught with uncertainty and the risk of misadven-ture, frustration, and failure, as Dewey put it. It's easy to see why many researchers would want to avoid the messy reality of doing, and so construct their theories in a better place: the perfect reality of a "pure knowing" constructed by reason. The difficulty is that the solutions, predictions, and explanations of one reality rarely fit the other. This may explain why, for example, the abstract economic theories conceived of by the brightest minds — and to which our political leaders hold onto like grim death — fail to explain the economic crisis that confronts us. The "key economic indicators" tell us that the economy is rebounding. Yet the experience of ordinary people indicates that we are in the midst of a serious depression (Bartlett & Steele, 1992; Saul, 1992).

Similarly, the rational solutions to the widely perceived failure of our schools to overcome the plague of social and economic problems that confront us — vouchers, competency testing, merit pay for teachers, higher standards, outcomes-based education, the testing of teachers, To-tal Quality Management (TQM), business partnerships, "schoolfare," the Regular Education Initiative — ultimately fail with students who do not grow up in the perfect reality imagined by planners and researchers. It may be rational, for example, to conclude that "competition brings out people's best," but the reality is that competition discourages many, if not most, students from trying at all (see Saul, 1992). It may be rational to assume that higher standards encourage students to "reach higher," but the reality is that higher standards necessarily increase the number of students who fail. (And, of course, higher standards begs the question: Whose standards?) It may also be rational to conclude that merit pay provides a powerful incentive to teachers to "do their best," but the reality is that teachers paid to increase the average performance of their class often give more attention to the brightest students, who are more likely to increase the class average (Shannon, 1988).

Solutions conceived of in the rational world of pure knowing just don't work in the messy, unpredictable, ambiguous, and uncertain reality in which we live. When I was a doctoral student at the University of Wisconsin, my linguistics professors often invoked the principle of Occam's Razor (John Occam was a 14th-century scholastic philosopher), which held that the simplest solution was always to be preferred. Recently I have begun to realize that Occam had it wrong. Simple solutions are to be preferred only in the rationally constructed reality of pure knowing, a reality that denies the complex lives of ordinary people living in the real world.

Perhaps the most egregious feature of the rational mind is its absolute intolerance for alternative points of view. This forecloses the possibility of original, creative solutions to the problems that confront us, solutions born of visceral or intuitive understandings. Men and women of reason simply dismiss these solutions as "irrational." Reason claims to place a premium on creative problem-solving, but the fervour with which it elevates method over content, how over why, reveals that for the rational mind, "creative problem-solving" is an oxymoron.

Reason's intolerance for nonrationality has a more sinister side, however. The struggle between rational and nonrational worldviews is not simply an academic debate about research methods or different points of view. Ultimately, it is about power, colonization, marginalization, and oppression. The quest for a certainty born of reason has resulted in many casualties. A critique of reason must, therefore, include consideration of moral and ethical issues.

Exalting How Over Why

The rational discourse of science has spilled over into everyday discourse(s) beyond the laboratory and the university (see Aronowitz, 1988).

The supremacy of reason (which sometimes goes by the name of logic) is unchallenged in the everyday affairs of ordinary people. Reason as *the* means for making sense of our world and solving the serious social, economic, and political problems we face is so taken for granted that it would not occur to most people that it could be challenged. It is assumed that the development of reason is the ultimate achievement of evolution, an achievement that sets us apart from other animals (though we scarcely see ourselves as animals) and our ancestors, whose worldviews were clouded by emotion and superstition.

Viewing reason as the product of thousands of years of evolution is, of course, self-serving, and it would be harmless in itself except for one thing: There are many people for whom reason (my dictionary defines *reason* as the ability "to analyze; think logically about; think out systematically," *Webster's*, 1960) is not their primary means of making sense of the world. If the development of reason is seen as an evolutionary development, then those people who do not "think logically about" are judged not to have developed to the same degree as those who think logically. It is only natural, then, that people who do not think rationally would be disadvantaged socially and economically. From this perspective, the nonrational person can never compete with the rational mind. This easily leads to the claim that elites earned their privileged place by virtue of their superior capacity for reason. (This natural right of elites to the lion's share of social goods recalls the "divine" right of kings to rule.)

The social Darwinist argument that naturalizes differential access to social goods (e.g., money, power, status) begins to fall apart when we acknowledge who is most likely to view the world through the lens of reason: white middle- and upper-class males. Valorizing reason has the effect of privileging those ways of knowing associated with dominant groups—again white middle- and upper-class males—while devaluing the ways of nondominant groups, often women and members of non-white and non-Western groups. As Elizabeth Ellsworth (1989) puts it: "Rational argument has operated in ways that set up as its opposite an irrational Other, which has been understood historically as the province of women and other exotic Others" (p. 301). Images of "irrational Others" are reinforced by media portrayals of, for example, women as "scatterbrained and illogical" (witness the continued popularity of *I Love Lucy* reruns), First Nations' people as superstitious, Asians as inscrutable, and the lives of urban Blacks as chaotic. By constructing Others as irrational, rational discourses permit us to marginalize whole groups of human beings—Blacks, Hispanics, First Nations people, women, gays, and lesbians—and blame them for their marginalization.

The logical solution, then, following this reasoning, to ameliorating the disadvantage and discrimination experienced by marginalized groups is to help them abandon their "irrational" ways and use reason to make their way in the world. Put a bit more crudely, if marginalized groups would just learn to be more like *us* (i.e., white middle-class males) they would be able to share in the cultural and economic riches of our society. Family literacy programs that are emerging throughout the United States and Canada as part of official efforts to combat the effects of poverty, for example, have less to do with teaching families to read than with teaching families to read like white middle-class people (Taylor, 1994).

In his story, Thomas Schwandt observes that the choice between methods is a moral decision. The rational method, by elevating how over why, masks the moral and ethical implications of method. This enables researchers to ask questions such as "Are Blacks as intelligent as whites?" or "Are women as good at problem-solving as men?" or "Should students with exceptionalities be integrated into regular classrooms?" and pretend that these questions are the product of cold, morally neutral logic. Elevating *how* over *why* also enables educators to implement testing and curricula derived from normative understandings of human beings without considering whose version of "normal" is privileged by school practices (*normal* usually means white, middle-class, Christian, male, and heterosexual [Ellsworth, 1989]).

Disputes about method distract people from the moral decisions being made (Fulcher, 1989). Method can never be separated from morality except in the socially constructed world of pure knowing imagined by reason. In the messy reality of people's real lives, method always involves assumptions about the way people live their lives and the way the (social) world ought to be (Gee, 1990; Schwandt, this volume). We therefore have an ethical obligation to examine the ideological assumptions—what James Gee calls "tacit theories"—underlying our choice of method and to consider who's interests are served by these choices. James Gee (1990) puts it this way: "One always has the (ethical) obligation to (try to) explicate . . . any theory that is (largely) tacit . . . when there is reason to believe that the theory advantages one's self or one's group over other people or other groups" (p. 22).

This second half of my story reflects the recent politicization of my work and so is part of my personal journey. I continue to be committed to improving the educational opportunities of students for whom learning to read and write is a struggle. I also remain committed to holistic, constructivist pedagogy that makes a place for learners' voices in our classrooms. But I also recognize that choice of method—reductionist versus constructivist practices, for example—is as political as it is pedagogical, involving decisions about people and the way they live their lives. I also understand that teaching practices, no matter how progressive, will always be insufficient for overcoming the social and economic conditions and institutional structures that produced so much failure in the first place. Literacy educators like me can never succeed in improving the lives of students disadvantaged by the effects of poverty and discrimination unless we find ways to challenge the racist, classist, sexist, homophobic, and ablist structures that ensure that many students achieve little economic or social success no matter how literate they become (see Gee, 1990; Taylor, 1994). Acknowledging the why of method demands nothing less.

A Long Road Ahead:
Contemplating the Future from the
Perspective of a Young Interpretist

Deborah J. Gallagher

> Between truth and lie are images and ideas we imagine and
> think are real, that paralyze our imagination and our thinking
> in our efforts to conserve them. We must continually learn to
> unlearn much of what we have learned, and learn to learn
> that we have not been taught. Only thus do we and our
> subject grow.
>
> —R. D. Laing (1972)

Although none of the contributors to this volume has reached the end of
her or his personal journey, our thoughts about what the future holds
for interpretive inquiry are likely to take on a different cast depending on
where we have been, how far we have come, and how far we have to go.
Most of those in whose company I now find myself are time-honored
travelers. All have, in my estimation, made eminent contributions to the
field of interpretive inquiry. Their work has made the road I have traveled thus far smoother and straighter than it would otherwise have been.

Were I to speculate about tomorrow from their vantage point, I
think my interest in the future would include considerations about the
legacy of my work. Will the contributions I have attempted to make lead
to meaningful, substantive changes? Or will the passing of time find
mainstream educational research continuing business as usual? I, like
everyone else, can only speculate about what it will be like in 100 years.
And like them, I have hopes and dreams. Unlike the others, though, I
have no legacy of consequence to consider, and a longer road stretches
before me chronologically. From this vantage point, I find myself won-

dering what kind of world I will be living in, at least in the next 30 years or so.

Am I optimistic or pessimistic? I would have to say both. From where I stand currently, the near future does not seem as full of promise as I would hope. My pessimism stems from what I perceive to be substantial resistance to the philosophical challenges facing the mainstream educational research community. Were this resistance overt, sparking heated debate and high-level intellectual discourse, I would be more sanguine. Instead, it seems that these challenges have been met with various forms of avoidance.

One form of avoidance, and the one I find most disturbing, is the bent toward recasting interpretive research as an alternative set of methods. This notion implicitly preserves the belief that methods can provide us with access to an independently existing reality. Interpretive research becomes a "softer" form of positivism, and in the process, its potential to transform is blunted if not lost altogether.

What is so disturbing is that it is difficult to detect the epistemological equivocation that has taken place in this line of reasoning. That which is familiar is seductive because it saves us from having to face the loss of security that comes with amending the way we have organized our world. So strong is the urge to preserve our "belief contexts" that we will do so without quite realizing it in any conscious way.

A second form of avoidance is to subjugate interpretive inquiry by conceiving of it as a complementary component of "real" research. In this manner, it becomes the handmaiden of the more dominant form of inquiry. I encountered this approach recently while listening to a researcher in a conference seminar that specifically addressed issues of method. While presenting his dissertation research, this researcher, who had completed his Ph.D. at one of the most respected institutions in the country, confidently explained that he had used qualitative methods as a portion of his work but had predominantly employed quantitative methods to ensure what he described as "the rigor of my research." Curious about this remark, I asked him why he believed that qualitative research lacked rigor. As he stumbled through a halfhearted retraction, his facial expression conveyed a sense of chagrin that he had committed a tactical error in assuming that his audience was composed entirely of rational people. Beyond attempting to save himself politically, he was not only unable but also uninterested in dealing with the question. One of my colleagues, who seemed equally confused, but more importantly, embarrassed by the query, quickly rescued him by changing the focus. Save for one other colleague whose eyes subtly met mine with a discerning glance, the remainder of the group seemed quite content to move on.

The above incident is not the only evidence I have noted toward making qualitative methods the "weak sister" (I use this term deliberately and with irony) of social sciences research. It seems not unusual anymore to read or attend presentations of research reports that proudly proclaim that " . . . both quantitative and qualitative methodologies [sic] were employed." And although our erstwhile candidate was one of the few I have heard express it overtly, I think that the "qualitative component" is widely assumed to be ornamentation to the traditionally dominant mode of research. Avoidance through subjugation seems to work well for many.

A third form of avoidance is to take the democratic approach. The reasoning of the realist goes something like this: "Everyone is entitled to his or her worldview. You can have yours, and I will have mine. Who can say that one is better than the other?" In a way, this is one of the best arguments because it at least tacitly acknowledges that decisions are involved in the *making* of one's belief context and that these decisions are moral rather than technical in nature. Yet it still fails to deal head on with the implications of this claim because the realist belief in truth as an independently existing entity doubles back on and subsequently subsumes the notion of moral decisionmaking. As a result, the realist stops short of examining, much less claiming responsibility for, both the intended and unintended consequences of embracing her or his own worldview.

I subscribe to a computer bulletin board that features discussions about education from a distinctly empiricist perspective. I don't participate in these discussions, but have found it interesting to read the exchanges about current issues that take place on this list. When Herrnstein and Murray's (1994) *The Bell Curve* was released, I logged onto the bulletin board eager to hear the discussion about this controversial book. I was surprised, but in retrospect should not have been, to encounter an eerie silence on the topic. My guess is that the active members of this list were deeply disturbed by the nature of the authors' assertions but were at a loss to come to terms with the book's empiricist claims, caught as they likely were between their instinctive sense that Hernstein and Murray created their conclusions and the realist belief that scientific methods discover the truth.

I have given a lot of thought as to why there continues to be avoidance of interpretivist principles. One explanation may lie in the constructivist theory of learning. At the center of this theory is the belief that learning is a process whereby new knowledge and experiences reconstruct current knowledge and experiences. This process takes place over time as new information disrupts current information. The critical aspects are time and the degree of incremental disruption. If the disruption of one's current knowledge or belief context is too abrupt or overwhelming, the individual naturally seeks some form of reconciliation. This, according to constructivist learning theory, is both a normal and predictable response because the human mind seeks to preserve a sense of equilibrium. We all do this. That is why, I think, we have individuals, many of whom would identify themselves as qualitative researchers, believing that empiricist and interpretist modes of inquiry are compatible or complementary.

As Heshusius (1989) explains it, "Paradigms do not offer 'right' and 'wrong' answers, nor perfect solutions. Rather, they provide sets of fundamental assumptions that are adequate (or no longer adequate) to generate the pertinent questions of the time and possibilities for their answers" (p. 411). She further explains that changes take place when it becomes more difficult to preserve current knowledge than it is to amend it. "The process of becoming self-conscious about our ultimate assumptions happens when the paradigm we unself-consciously live in reaches its limitations" (Heshusius, 1989, p. 403). My hope for the future is that more of us will embrace rather than avoid challenges to our belief contexts, deliberately recognizing and addressing the limitations of our current understanding. This is a difficult endeavor, but one that I think is not impossible because, paradoxically, the same need for equilibrium that on the one hand seems to result in avoidance becomes the very thing that moves us forward.

But before I become too hopeful, I must note what I consider to be a troubling dimension of our human nature, one that I think bodes ill for future prospects. The dimension I refer to is our propensity to fear and subsequently reject freedom. Even in the face of outcomes or circumstances that provide painful evidence of substantial incongruity, we seek unselfconsciously to avoid rather than resolve the contradiction.

In his exploration of Nazism and authoritarianism, *Escape from Freedom*, Erich Fromm (1964) provides a compelling explication of how human beings seek exoneration from responsibility in exchange for giving up personal freedom. This personal flight from freedom is also the theme of literature as well as the world's great philosophies and religions. I deeply suspect that, although we rarely acknowledge it, we want so desperately to avoid making choices because we intuitively realize that any choice we make involves a necessary tradeoff between more or less undesirable outcomes. And so we cling desperately to the belief that somewhere out there there is some grand mediator between ourselves and our choices, call it truth, reality, empiricism, or what have you.

This is, of course, a nonsolution, and it has occurred to me that we assume this stance when we *seem* to stand to gain the most from maintaining the current state of affairs. The terrible irony of this lies in the short-term sense that self-interest is in diametrical conflict with the interests of others. Perhaps the solution is the ability to see that what is in the interests of others is also in the interest of ourselves. It requires tremendous courage to transcend the immediacy of our existences and the illusion of our separateness from others. I am uncertain about how much hope I can place in our human capacity to marshal such courage on a large enough scale to make fundamental changes within the next 50 years or so.

Interpretive inquiry asks courage of us. Primarily, its principles require us to face ourselves and each other, a situation that impels us to account more honestly for our personal use of power. No longer are we able to claim that our moral decisions are not really our own but rather "just the way things are." We have to admit to schoolchildren and their parents that the injustices that occur in our schools are the result of choices we have made. They in turn can challenge us; and, quite frankly, I think we find many of our choices to be indefensible once we are able to see them in a different light. In short, we have to give up much of our control and authority.

In a related vein, those of us in higher academia would no longer be guaranteed the right to be listened to on the basis of our credentials and the appropriation of exclusive methods of inquiry. Rather, we would be judged on the basis of our wisdom, insight, and integrity—characteristics to which we cannot lay exclusive claim nor reproduce in others whom we choose to anoint.

Finally, I think life in academia would require far more of us individually in terms of time and physical, intellectual, and emotional energy. In a recent fleeting exchange with a colleague in which we were both lamenting our lack of time, I spoke of how time- (not to mention emotionally and intellectually) consuming it is to be a member of a dissertation committee when the doctoral student is conducting a qualitative dissertation. She offered me a triumphant grin and advised me that "Maybe you ought to rethink all that qualitative stuff."

This conversation left me reflecting on my situation as a young interpretive researcher. I have realized that to do high-caliber interpretive work requires the total person rather than simply the skilled execution of research methods. For me, this means that I spend a lot of time thinking about who I am and what I believe. I no longer have the luxury of taking issues at surface value. It has taken me a long time to work through philosophical issues such that I am able to make a contribution I can consider to be of substance to the profession. In short, being an interpretive inquirer is not about what you do; it is about who you are.

When incidents such as the ones I describe above occur, I am left with the feeling that there is a wide gulf between myself and the other person that I would very much like to bridge. Will such gulfs be bridged in the course of my career? I hope so. This is not to say that I want everyone to be of the same mind, but rather that we become more comfortable with each others' minds in attempting to come to some consensus about our guiding assumptions. On the one hand, I see evidence that we are moving forward, however slow that movement seems to be. On the other hand, I am apprehensive that our fear of freedom and responsibility will preclude such progress. Whatever the outcome, I think that I have a long and interesting road ahead of me.

In my ideal vision of the future, our work in educational inquiry would be judged primarily on its depth of discernment and its facility to enlighten, with the idea in mind that it should lead directly and substantially to more satisfying lives for all schoolchildren.

For this to happen, I think we must openly acknowledge the hermeneutical nature of social inquiry. Our work should involve honest efforts to understand each other's perspectives. In short, understanding would be a highly esteemed value among us. Achieving greater depths of understanding means that we have the courage to let go of what we think we know so that we can grow and move forward. It also means that we have the courage to be responsible for our freedom to make choices as individuals and as a community. This, I think, will be the real beginning of the future I would like to look toward.

Commentary

EGON G. GUBA

As I read the contributions of other chapter authors and reread my own, I was struck by the ever-continuing development that the authors document. Wherever we may have been in the past, we are somewhere else now, and surely will be somewhere else again in the future. If, as these statements suggest, we are currently witnessing an unfolding of new conceptions (paradigms?) about our research methods, our disciplines, the nature of knowledge broadly conceived, and ourselves, it is clear that we all expect that unfolding to continue for yet a long time. Indeed, I am sure that if the wishes of these several authors were controlling, that unfolding would never cease, for if it did, the development of new, more sophisticated understandings would halt. All views are soon emptied of their possibilities; the hope for the future rests on the ongoing invention of new views that raise new questions and propose new ways to pursue them.

Where Have We Been?

Most of the contributors — researchers, teachers, professors, therapists — document a movement from what may be described as the "received view" (Guba) or the "classic science view" (Rhodes) to "paradigm change" (Ballard, Israelite). Their designating term for their own original view varies: *positivist* or *logical positivist* (Guba, Poplin); *behaviorist* (Dudley-Marling, Israelite, Poplin); *determinist* (Dudley-Marling); *reductionist* (Gallagher, Poplin); and *mechanist* (Gallagher). They also use terms such as *"hard" science, orthodoxy, scientism, objectivism, mathematical modeling, statistics, measurement, quantitative research, experimentalism, technical, orderly, hierarchical,* and *context-free* to describe aspects of that view, whether their primary commitments were to inquiry, teaching, or therapy. Taken as a group, these terms represent the paradigm to which all were either initially socialized or toward which they were pointed in their training, but which all have come to reject for one reason or another.

Three of the contributors assert that they had never been adherents of this received view. Heshusius is outspoken in denying that she was ever a positivist, and states that she rejects the mechanistic paradigm. Schwandt disavows a turnabout, claiming to have been unschooled in the debates over methodology; his thinking, he avers, is the product of two cultures: science *and* the humanities. Smith suggests that he was never "deeply socialized into [the] 'technical' mode." All three of these authors make clear, however, that they likewise reject this paradigm; having been exposed to it, they found it wanting.

Why Did These Contributors Reject the Received View?

Each of the contributed papers may be taken as a case report from an author about her or his own personal experience of rejection. They differ, of course. But rejection seems not to have occurred abruptly. Dudley-Marling notes that his move to a holistic framework was gradual, with no "defining moment," "crucial insight," or "aha's." Gallagher comments that "only after a number of years . . . did I begin to have glimmers of the possibility that [the] reductive approach was flawed." Rhodes observes that his shift away from the "classic scientific view of reality . . . was a gradual process."

For those contributors claiming never to have been adherents to classical positivism, there occurred not a transformation but rather a validation or confirmation of what had been believed all along, and tenaciously maintained despite the assaults of a culture rooted in the received view. Thus Heshusius affirms that her particular background made her different from those who had had to shift fundamental assumptions: "I never believed in [the positivist worldview] in the first place." Yet she felt unsettled by her experiences in graduate school, and only after her seminar experience with a liberating professor did she feel that she was "no longer forced to pretend that the unreal life is real."

In another scenario, Schwandt asserts that he "did not arrive at graduate school wearing the cloak of neobehaviorist, neopositivist, empiricist, what have you," not because he had some other paradigmatic commitment but because he had been trained in the humanities and thus had not been exposed to the received view in any depth. But over time, a series of experiences led him to evolve a unique position, a "union of moral and cognitive concerns" that stands as much in opposition to the old science as those of any of the other contributors. However the belief systems of the contributors evolved, there are several themes that recur as reasons for the changes each of them underwent.

Contributors often felt a sense of alienation or estrangement that was not an intellectual response but one of feelings and emotions. Heshusius reports a disjunction between her graduate school courses and other experiences that were at odds with her own natural knowledge. She felt that graduate study was a sterile experience. Poplin judged that graduate school nurtured only a narrow part of her intellect. Ballard noted his struggle with the idea that he should try to separate his research from his personal beliefs, and decided to stop pretending that he could. Anglin simply gave up on the world of statistics, which he found trivial and divorced from any reality that was meaningful to him. It had made him feel crazy and incompetent.

Emotional knowing was central. Dudley-Marling felt "uncomfortable" with behaviorism, leading to a sense of ambiguity, contradiction, and uncertainty. Gallagher experienced a "feeling of constant struggle," but felt "relieved and vindicated" later. In a similar vein, reading a reference by Rorty "felt right" to Smith. Ballard reports missing a sense of the "delight of this work" when he wrote "journal accounts of behaviors observed and changed"; he found "real science" neither humane nor interesting. Heshusius found herself dazed, shocked, stunned, isolated, and confused on being exposed to the received view in her early graduate studies, leaving her feeling depressed, powerless, and desperate. Smith reports such a violent reaction of avoidance that he could not bring himself to read the professional quantitative literature. I myself could not believe that my first field study, Project Discovery, was so roundly rejected by critics when I and the study's audiences had found it so useful, evocative, and impressive. Poplin was sure that there were many "unnamed" problems that she intuitively recognized but could not cast into traditional form.

The contributors also show remarkable consistency in judging the received view as too acontextual and reductive. Both Dudley-Marling and Gallagher railed against research done in contrived or experimental rather than natural or "real-life" settings. Similarly, Heshusius argues that rational constructions are severed from real life. Dudley-Marling further noted that conventional research placed too much focus on similarities while excluding differences. Gallagher complains that reductionism screens context, making it relatively inaccessible, noting that "forcing our world into a neat package just [doesn't work]." I myself noted the enormous gap between theory and practice. Rhodes suggests that he came to "envision life as a human/nonhuman network of interchanging systems," and to "celebrate child deviance as the preservation of an open, evolving human ecology."

Contributors sensed a major hiatus between old views of research and teaching, on the one hand, and their understanding of human learning and experience. Both Ballard and Heshusius take exception to animal research (rats and pigeons) taken as equivalent, or at least parallel, to human research. Poplin concludes from her experience as a journal editor that virtually nothing in journal articles is productive in "real lives." Heshusius decries the piecemeal nature of most human research. And Israelite realized that even pizza and Monopoly could not replace reality.

Contributors also sensed major methodological problems with old-view research and teaching. Dudley-Marling and Gallagher think there is an overemphasis on quantification. Anglin discovered that even a survey is not innocent. I myself felt that in a study of knowledge production and utilization in schools of education throughout the country, by far the most useful information was gleaned from a small number of site visits as compared to the literally thousands of survey questionnaires completed by professors, deans, and other administrators. Dudley-Marling pointed to the impossibility of an objective inquiry (a cardinal old-view principle), and Rhodes noted that the "me" and "not-me" are less clearly delineated in the new view than would have been contemplated under the old. Heshusius felt that often the wrong questions were being asked: "how" rather than "why" questions.

Common among the contributors was a sense that research, teaching, and therapy are all political and moral events, despite the claim of value freedom maintained within the old view. Ballard says that the acknowledgment of values was missing in the old approach, and Schwandt sees a return to morality as indispensable to resolving many of the old-view problems. The question of voice came up: Heshusius felt that the voices of students, or the voices of institutionalized people, were simply not reflected in theories of research or practice. Ballard points to the disjunction between ordinary people's lives and their representation as research subjects. Gallagher believes students are made to feel incompetent and powerless. She warns us to mistrust the easy power of "order without permission," and to guard against the implied privilege of researchers and teachers by their maintenance of hierarchy and exclusivity. Similarly, Schwandt reports that he came to appreciate the existence of orthodoxy ("catechisms of . . . believers") and a "politics of method" as he worked with graduate students, indicative, he says, of the strong but unreflective commitment of traditional faculty (he labels their stance a "caricature" of commitment).

Finally, some of the contributors report having been influenced in their shift (or reaffirmation) by, as Poplin expresses it, becoming familiar with other worldviews. I myself was overwhelmed by the implications of Thomas Kuhn's *The Structure of Scientific Revolutions* (1970). Rhodes indicates that his thinking was greatly influenced when he became aware of the "new physics": Bell's nonlocal reality, "quantum weirdness," and similar concepts. Schwandt professes to have been greatly influenced by his coursework at Indiana, with me and in philosophy of science, statistics, measurement, and experimental design, and by reports of graduate students in my own informal seminar concerning the problems they were encountering with their professors. Smith reports that his reading of Rorty's *Philosophy and the Mirror of Nature* (1979) piqued his curiosity and led him to read Bernstein, Putnam, Gadamer, Giddens, and others.

Where Are the Contributors Now?

The present state of mind of the contributors is reflected both in the terms they currently use to portray themselves, as well as in their descriptions of their new attitudes or action patterns. In the first case, Ballard sees himself as "open to a range of interpretations, constructions, and reconstructions," learning through participation with others. Dudley-Marling uses the term *interpretist*, but also claims a holistic posture. Heshusius and Smith also subscribe to the terms *interpretation* or *interpretive*, while Poplin sees in herself elements of holism, feminism, and constructivism. I myself am committed to the constructivist label. Rhodes describes himself as a constructivist and a postmodernist. It is certainly the case that each of these terms represents different shades of meaning, even when the same term is used by different contributors, but all of them represent a disavowal of the received-view labels with which they characterized their initial positions.

New attitudes display a similar variation. Ballard indicates that he is welcoming "uncertainty and complexity." Dudley-Marling sees himself as "willing to relinquish precision and control" and to "live with uncertainty," despite the fact that he experiences "lingering contradictions." Gallagher sees herself as more trusting of her instincts and more "unperturbed by the challenges [of] the interpretive paradigm." I myself experienced feelings of "doubt, insecurity, and anxiety," especially about whether I might not be misleading students and colleagues, but also found myself less willing to extend special privilege to practitioners of the received view.

Emergent allegiance to new paradigm viewpoints is perhaps best characterized by actions the contributors report themselves taking now.

Dudley-Marling finds himself "embracing qualitative methods" and, perhaps more importantly, "strengthening [his own] writer's voice" and "politicizing my work." Israelite welcomes holistic and sociocultural perspectives. Heshusius indicates that she has become a student of "paradigmatic underpinnings." Similarly, Poplin has become a student of new approaches, and now seeks to "nourish . . . teachers' own institutions and energy." Rhodes has adopted a new paradigmatic view of reality and epistemology, a paradigm that "allows the final erasure of the line between science and literature, science and art." Schwandt reports that he is engaged in exploring the act of inquiry as an emotional and moral as well as an intellectual cognitive activity, in examining the relation of self, other, the world, the union of intellect and passion, thought and feeling, and in working on the question of "how shall I *be* toward these people I am studying?" Surely these statements would sound very odd to the scientist committed to the received view; nothing better illustrates the movement of these contributors to a view very unrelated to the accepted view of the past.

Where Are We Going?

Given these dramatic changes, what will the future be like in the eyes of these contributors? Ballard believes in a dialectic between "the ways we imagine that the world is and could be" that will both define problems and lead to their solutions. Dudley-Marling hopes for a "more just and equitable world to live in." Gallagher sees us involved in a "journey worth making" and one that she, at least, will "continue to make." I myself foresee a "continuing revolution," one that will lead to a "future that [is] . . . even better informed and sophisticated" than present views. Heshusius looks forward to a future that she cannot foretell at this time, but she intends to "be more conscious of the process of change as it happens," and expresses delight that the "(re)turn to interpretation . . . has made it easier to do so." Poplin expects that "so many things that are obscured from myself [now] . . . will be interpreted or reinterpreted later," and declares herself ready to "take another leap in my own personal and professional journey." Schwandt sees himself "on a journey," one that he expects to continue.

What does all this add up to? While the development of their present state of mind has followed a unique path for each of the contributors, I see in each a struggle to integrate their theories of research, of teaching, of therapy, or whatever with their everyday experiences, to resolve the conflicts and dilemmas sensed by bringing their constructs and experiences together in the terms of a consistent worldview — a consistent way of "making sense" of what they feel and what they believe. I would call those views their preferred paradigms. The discontinuities and disjunctions that each felt between what they had been taught or urged to do in the received view and what they found practically useful and meaningful to do were too great to ignore, too painful to be allowed to continue, too ineffective to reach the (different) goals to which each aspired. Each responded by defining (even if only tacitly and incompletely) a preferred paradigm in ways that made sense to them in their own contexts, that resolved or at least ameliorated the sensed conflicts and dilemmas. They were uniform in rejecting received wisdom, but divergent in settling on (for them) acceptable alternatives.

My own hopes for the future of educational research are not inconsistent with these sentiments. I can capture these hopes in three words: *decentralized, deregulated*, and *cooperative*. Educational research has, in the main, failed because within the rubrics of the received model, we have believed in the possibility of generalized, one-size-fits-all solutions to educational problems. Innovations proved effective by the methods of science would have general applicability. But the new ways of thinking reflected in these pages make clear that solutions to problems must be developed and applied locally to have any chance of success. Research must be decentralized to the local context.

Second, research and researchers must be freed from the strictures of a prescribed one "right" way to achieve truth and knowledge. Inquiry must be deregulated from the rules of the game embodied in the received view, and venture into ways of generating knowledge that reflect our new philosophical commitments. We cannot, as someone once said, put new wine into old bottles.

Third, research must be carried out cooperatively; that is, with the full consent and involvement of the persons affected in any way by the outcomes. We can no longer tolerate the exclusion of stakeholders from an integral role in the development of knowledge; to do so is not only immoral but ultimately counterproductive. Those who lack ownership in knowledge feel under no obligation to be ruled by it. Inquiry that is coercive can have no privilege.

On Tending Broken Dreams

Lous Heshusius

What do I wish for the future of educational thought and research? Which reimaginings might benefit the well-being of our grandchildren and great-grandchildren? In responding to these questions, I can no longer separate what is important in my own life from what is important to "the field." I tried to engage in such separation during my training in traditional research, although I always *did* wonder who, or what, "the field" was, and how values concerning "it" could somehow be different from values concerning my own life. Given this starting point, I would like to ponder what I see as urgent issues for the future.

Causes of Disorder: Living a Reality Promised by Another

> But it is a mistake this extreme position, this orderly and military progress; a convenience, a lie. There is always deep below it, even when we arrive punctually at the appointed time with our white waist-coats and polite formalities, a rushing stream of broken dreams, nursery rhymes, street cries, half finished sentences and sights.

Virginia Woolf (1931, p. 219), in *The Waves*, tells the tale of dissociation: the leading of a life in which underneath the formalized surfaces runs a "rushing stream" of nonrational and tacit knowing that we can ignore only at great cost. Several stories in Chapter 2 variously describe the frustration, boredom, avoidance, guilt, and the sense of despair that occurred when trying to adhere to the "orderly progress" and "polite formalities" of positivist thought. The primary cause of disorder, as Jiddu Krishnamurti (e.g., 1954, 1972) reminds us, is believing a reality promised by another. Positivism promised a reality by way of a strictly formulated methodology. It ran up against our "broken dreams" and "half finished sentences." We can't get away from ourselves.

Fortunately, today's cultural and intellectual climate is informed by many diverse perspectives ranging from feminist, deconstructionist, and reconstructionist thought to the increasing influence of indigenous worldviews, the call for the ecological imperative in education (Bowers, 1993), and efforts to explore what connections between Eastern and Western thought might mean for the social sciences (Kalamaras, 1994; Varela et al., 1993). Within or extending from these critically creative and expansive positions, we should be able to find or to create a home compatible with our own lives.

On Body, Mind, and Emotion

Referring to Gregory Bateson's work, Mary Catherine Bateson (1977, p. 61) says of emotive life:

> . . . the emotions, those things that we are accustomed to regard as rather amorphous and unintellectual—indeed, as interfering with the effective pursuit of intellect—are the partial perceptions in consciousness of highly precise and patterned forms of computations. . . . "The heart has its reasons which the reason does not at all perceive."

And in his classic book on the subjugation of the body, Francis Barker (1984, p. 63) observes:

> Neither wholly present, nor wholly absent, the body is confined, ignored, exscribed from discourse, and yet remains at the edge of visibility, troubling the space from which it has been banned.

In our stories, the frustration with and avoidance of our work, the rumblings of Egon Guba's belly, the exhaustion Deborah Gallagher still feels just thinking about her reductionistic past, Neita Israelite's not feeling good, my own sudden weariness and exhaustion when confronted with positivist and behaviorist practices—these bodily and emotive manifestations of disturbances kept " . . . troubling the space from which [they had] been banned."

In foregrounding the body as a vital and primary source of knowing, we have, as Berman (1984, p. 179) states, "made sensual or affective science theoretically possible." To be fully present in a situation, says Saleebey (1992, p. 114), demands sensuous attendance, for the body knows context in a way that the intellect does not. How, then, can we bring the somatic and emotive substrata to the foreground to transcend modernity's alienated and alienating consciousness? How can we engage in sensuous inquiry? Telling interior stories as we do in Chapter 2 is one way. We should, however, not have to wait until years after such knowledge has made itself felt.

How to attend sensuously to our work will be asking something new from social researchers. Saleebey (1992, p. 116) suggests that we engage in various practices (e.g., meditation, relaxation) that sharpen awareness of mind–body integrity. I would not wish to equate, however, the process of integrating the divided self with a set of practices, however beneficial. Practices for mind–body integration may bring about integrated attentiveness during practice time. This does not guarantee, however, that such attentiveness will see us through the day. At a deeper level there needs to exist the willingness in all we do to let the mind rest in the body, its original home, not from exhaustion, not for direct sensual pleasure, not for dulling relaxation, not to perfect bodily performances — but for a heightened state of integrated attentiveness.

I do not claim this achievement, and am painfully aware that we "write ourselves into being," a phrase I borrow from where I don't know. What we write rarely indicates where we are, but rather what we long for and struggle with. The challenge of embodying ourselves and our work is immense. As Saleebey and Weick (1994, p. 13) observe, the language we have for talking of bodily matters is conceptually limited and pale: In thinking about the body, it is not even certain if we have expressed what we mean. Moreover, they state, the moment we talk about the "body" we immediately are drawn into awareness of our own bodies, which is often a trying and even frightening experience. But in the end it is far more destructive to be out of touch with our bodies and with emotive life.

Reconstructing the Selfother or the Otherself

Our stories show, I believe, that the authors are as concerned with reconstructing as they are with deconstructing. Various writers have cast postmodern thought into two major molds: the deconstruction of the possibility of an "objective" representation of reality — and therefore of self and of other — and the reconstruction (not representation) of it. Some see deconstruction as limited, abstract, and reactionary, a logical extension of modernity that perpetuates the focus on ultimate disconnectedness (Griffin, 1988; Spretnik, 1991; Waugh, 1989). Others believe that both deconstruction and reconstruction are necessary parts of postmodern life; it is in the *re*constructive mode, however, that the possibility for a healing future is seen to exist (see Gablik, 1991; Keller, 1988; Tarnas, 1991). Because of the mandate to endlessly demystify, deconstructionist proposals have, with rare exceptions (see Kalamaras, 1994, Chapter 7), offered no framework for integrating the divided self. Some proponents of reconstructionist thought, on the other hand, point to the need to overcome the conceptual internal divisions of mind, body, and emotion while making both social and ecological connectivity the central ground for scholarship, for action, for art, for our lives. In doing so, they express a particular direction within both feminist and ecological thought which Catherine Keller (1988, p. 218) calls a "hermeneutics of connection."

I felt a strong desire in our stories to transcend modernity's alienating consciousness. The reconnecting with one's somatic and emotive knowing, the search for connection with other cultures, the return to the humanities and the arts, the searching of what one's human (as opposed to methodological) relationship with those we "study" should be, the personal honesty with which the stories are told—all of these not only demystify but also replace the desire inherent in Western rationality to separate and control with a search for shared consciousness and shared purpose.

The desire to transcend an alienating consciousness begs for the reimagining not only of the boundaries we draw between mind, body, and emotions, but also of those we draw between the self and both the human and nonhuman other. Autonomy and individuality, the pillar of the enlightenment project, must be problematized and reconstructed within the larger participatory consciousness of the "hermeneutics of connection," where the self and other are seen, not as separate entities, but as an ontological and epistemological unity. This mode of consciousness is reflected in Gregory Bateson's (1972) work on the ecology of mind; in indigenous worldviews; in various aspects of Eastern thought; in feminist thought that emphasizes radical relatedness as outlined by Gablik (1991), Keller (1988), Rose (1994), and Waugh (1989); and in today's theoretical physics (Bohm, 1980).

Rereading my own story, I was struck by the sentence "I had learned nothing about *them*, and therefore learned nothing about myself." Or so I thought. I was referring to the masses of data I had gathered in graduate school on the "phenomena" of mental retardation, data that had told me nothing about the real persons inside those we label retarded. Writing that sentence, I had not been thinking explicitly about the concept of selfother unity, but I was implying just that: the "other" is an inextricable part of the "me." The other is who we define ourselves against. Research is not excluded from this human process of needing an other against whom to define a self. This includes researchers and theorists who engage in qualitative and interpretive inquiry and who, as I suggest else-where (Heshusius, 1994), maintain the self–other distance, defining self against other. Often, those we study live in the realm of what we don't want to identify with, what we are fearful of, what we don't want to imagine for ourselves, what inconveniences us. We then define all of that as other. This allows us to address through formal study what we don't accept as a possibility for our own lives without having to acknowledge these reactions as our own. As Catherine Keller (1988, p. 79) says: "Every self . . . posits the Other as an object, an opponent, in order to become itself."

The other "is the shadow of the Western mind," says Jurgen Kremer (1992, p. 175). It is in the other where we find what has been excommunicated from intimate participation: " . . . the feminine, wilderness, and 'strange' cultures" (p. 175). Understanding how an entire civilization could banish animals to zoos and Indians to reservations and plunk five-year-old children down in front of computers, says Morris Berman (1984, p. 343), "is to come to terms with how fucked up we really are, and at least open up the possibility for somatic reconstruction."

We can add to the list of what has been distanced from the self: nature we gain mastery over and confine to conservation areas; Black persons we banished into slavery; old persons we isolate in nursing homes; young children we have to place in day care; gay and lesbian persons we refuse to see; the homeless we learn to step over; the "re-tarded" we place in segregated settings; the "learning disabled" we send to school basements or portables; the "gifted" we send to "enrichment" programs; the "behavior disordered" we place in behavior management classes; and "research subjects" we run through experiments and reduce to statistics. I am sure there are additional excommunicated others, some still in the closet, transferences of our somatic and emotional shadows.

I now realize that I *was* learning a lot about myself in graduate school while busily amassing "data." Under the guise of objectivity, the self and other were deeply connected in an underhanded manner: I was constructing a relationship with the other in which I posited myself as unrelated, normal, separate, disembodied, and in control, "researching" the "not-me." For as Berman (1984, pp. 178–179) says, "Only a disembodied intellect can confront 'matter,' 'data,' or 'phenomena'—loaded terms that Western culture uses to maintain the subject/object distinction."

The extraordinary attempt in the social sciences under positivist dogmas to separate what can't be separated, to split other and self, resulted in a thin and bloodless concept of self and therefore of other, so vividly described in several of our stories. I believe we are still in the middle of becoming conscious of just how far we went and how much it is still with us. I hope there will come a time when the concept and the reality of selfother unity will be the taken-for-granted basis for all our work, so that peace and ecological health may be more easily fostered as forms of radical empathy. Anything that education and educational research can do to foster such participatory consciousness will be a great gain. We and the youngsters in our care may then gain insight into "other" by seeing her, him, or it as an intimate part of ourselves that needs to see the light of day. Such understanding will undoubtedly raise new questions about ourselves, questions that, paradoxically, to use James Baldwin's (1961, p. 13) words, will "illuminate the world":

> The question which one asks oneself begins, at last, to illuminate the world, and becomes one's key to the experience of others. One can only face in others what one can face in oneself. On this confrontation depends the measure of our wisdom and compassion.

From Moral Discourse to Moral Life

When the self and other are seen as belonging to the same consciousness, all living is moral. Then, epistemological choices are no longer rational choices that presuppose the possibility of legitimately separating the rational from the nonrational and discourse from actual living. The influential writings by Richard Rorty (1979, 1982), for instance, define moral discourse in terms of what a community of inquiry, in rational solidarity, agrees upon by way of setting forth a good argument. If I force myself into an abstract academic mindset I can, perhaps, intellectually agree. But when I close the book I find myself asking: What does all of this *mean*? Did Rorty influence me to see myself in the particulars of my real-life day-to-day behavior? Did he bring me in relation to my somatic and emotive life, where the moral questions are lodged? Did he bring me in relation to action? To other? I find I cannot affirm any of these questions. Instead I see people sitting around a table, engaged in moral discourse, negotiating toward a rational agreement. I want to ask them: What do you do? How does this translate into living? How would the self be involved and changed? How would the self and other unite, or separate? How would one's bodily and emotive life be involved? My sense is that they have not thought about these questions. I feel disembodied once more. I don't feel, see, sense, touch moral life. I hear discourse only. I can forget.

To live morally requires, in the first instance, not moral discourse, but a relentless awareness of ourselves in the particulars of moment-to-moment living. In the stories of struggle and change as recounted in this book, I read of complexities and moral dilemmas in the sorting and resorting of the self–other relationship in actual pedagogical and research settings, as these dilemmas play themselves out in concrete events as well as internally, where the moral questions exist most deeply. I feel the others' struggle, the guilt, the doubt, the longing. By comparison, rational, intellectual arguments temporarily intrigue me but do not penetrate the rest of my life: I am untouched. I remain unmoved. Dissociation continues. "Broken dreams" and "half-finished sentences" keep tugging, this time, at my moral life.

On Tending the Divided Self

The collective search in our stories can be characterized, I believe, by the phrase Mary Poplin uses to describe hers: It reflects a searching for a "compatibility with life" after having been severed from it for too long. One could ask: How will we know if compatibility with life is present? What are its indicators? Is it enough to know it for oneself? Do the reader who reads us and the students we teach need to feel and know it as well? Should we even try to identify and characterize "compatibility with life"? Should it remain tacit? Where does compatibility with life take place: in reflecting on one's past, in experiencing the present, in imagining the future?

But we *do* know when we read or hear someone whether compatibility with life is present. Ralph Waldo Emerson (in Richardson, 1990, p. 116) says:

> Only so much do I know, as I have lived. Instantly we know whose words are loaded with life, and whose not. . . . Whenever the pulpit is usurped by a formalist, then is the worshipper defrauded and disconsolate. We shrink as soon as the prayers begin. . . . [The preacher] has lived in vain. He [sic] had not one word intimating that he had laughed or wept, was married or in love, had been commended, or cheated, or chagrined. If he had ever lived and acted, we were none the wiser for it. . . . Not one fact in all his experience had he yet imported into his doctrine. This man had ploughed and planted and talked and bought and sold; he had read books, he had eaten and drunken; his head aches, his ear throbs; he smiles and suffers; yet was there not a surmise, a hint, in all the discourse, that he had ever lived at all. Not a line did he draw out of real history . . . it could not be told from his sermon . . . whether he had a father or a child . . .

whether he was a citizen or a country man; or any other fact of his biography. It seemed strange that people should come to church. It seemed as if their houses were very unentertaining, that they should prefer his thoughtless clamor.

Positivism brought lifeless and thoughtless clamor. Formalist clamor in other guises, however postmodern, may also be promising realities superimposed, methodologized, and alienating. At least one response to the question of how not to become dissociated is contained in Emerson's message: our words need to be "loaded with life." Our words as educators and educational researchers should never make the reader wonder if we had lived at all.

Using Susan Griffin's (1984, p. 175) words, then, we learn, very young, to disown a part of our own being and trade our real existence for a delusion: "We grow used to ignoring the evidence of our own experience, what we hear or see, what we feel in our own bodies." This dissociation within externalizes into many destructive ways. Awareness of this dividedness within will need to be the neverending starting point for its healing. I believe this to be a major task for education and educational research: to live and work *within* such awareness rather than contribute to its suppression. For myself, putting this book together has created an opportunity to work within it.

Social Science Research in 2044: Coequality, or Still Nasty After All Those Years

NEITA KAY ISRAELITE

"Almost no one in the academic world denies that professorial nasti-ness—intense ever since universities were founded in the Middle Ages—has never been more vicious than it is today," *New York Times* educa-tion reporter William Honan said in the summer of 1994 (p. 38).

In explaining why, Honan suggested, it is important to understand the tradition from which such strong emotions arise:

> Georges May, a former provost, dean and professor of French at Yale University, said academic disputes had always been heated because professors believed they are engaged in the search for truth, and those who claim to seek the truth are quick to find the infidels.
> "The university is a daughter of the church," he said. "We have inherited from it the costumes, the vocabulary and the concern for truth, and when the truth is at stake you may regard someone who disagrees with you as a heretic." (Honan, 1994, p. 38)

As May notes, the world of the church and the world of academia share some important commonalities. One quality alluded to, but not explicitly mentioned, is that both institutions have established or pre-scribed codes of behavior that its members are expected to observe. Anyone who has ever attended a typical university commencement has experienced costumes, vocabulary, and ritual ceremony mindful of reli-gious events. Indeed, orthodoxy, that is, conformity to the approved form of a doctrine, philosophy, or ideology, is an expectation, if not a requirement, of many academic environments.

May refers to the university as a "daughter of the church." On the surface, feminization of the term "university" is curious when one considers that throughout history most professors and administrators have been male. On closer examination, however, one realizes that patriarchal language always feminizes entities traditionally controlled by men, be they ships, cars, countries, or universities.

There are strong similarities between the patriarchal nature of the church and the patriarchal nature of academia. In both institutions, men have long been in collective positions of power that have enabled them to develop language, knowledge, and values in patriarchal forms that have excluded women (O'Brien, 1990). Men have used their positions to define what we know, how we come to know it, and who judges its worth. Both institutions traditionally have held that there is but one truth or objective reality, be it based on the Bible or on scientific rationality.

Who, then, are the infidels? Those who do not conform; those who want to look at things differently. It is the infidel who has seen the need for a fundamentally different understanding of the world. It is the infidel who has argued that personal reality is a complex and ever-changing social construction evolving through the process of human interaction. It is the infidel who has called for reform in research practices. From this perspective, being labelled an infidel places one in good company.

Research with Persons Who Are Deaf and Hard of Hearing

To be asked what I wish for the future of social science research came at a time when I was reflecting on my professional life working with persons who are deaf and hard of hearing. One of the important readings I came across was Shulamit Reinharz's (1992) book, *Feminist Methods in Social Research*, which has become a major influence on the perspectives I now hold on the future of research in my field. Feminist methods are applicable to fields where groups of people have been marginalized or ignored, and where unequal power and status relations exist. One such field is surely my own.

The fields of education and rehabilitation of persons who are deaf and hard of hearing have long been dominated by archetypal patriarchal beliefs. In addition to and overlapping with these beliefs is the influence of the deficit-driven medical model. "This model has the assumption that differences in physical, sensory or mental capabilities necessarily produce a defective member of society" (Kyle & Pullen, 1988, p. 50). From this perspective, being deaf or hard of hearing traditionally has been seen as a pathology to be fixed or cured.

The influence of medical model thinking has had a negative impact on many dimensions of the lives of persons who are deaf and hard of hearing. For instance, discriminatory training, hiring, and promotion practices have created a tradition of underemployment in teaching and other career areas. There also has been limited participation in educational policymaking and pedagogy.

In recent years, a shift has started to occur in how we think, talk, and write about persons who are deaf and hard of hearing. The recognition of a distinctly deaf culture and community, acknowledgment of American Sign Language as a legitimate natural language instead of a telegraphic form of English, and the growing acceptance of deaf persons as members of a cultural and linguistic minority reflect the beginnings of a change in the power and status relationship between the hearing majority and the deaf minority. For instance, the "Deaf President Now" (DPN) movement in 1988 at Washington's Gallaudet University, the first and only liberal arts university for deaf people in the world, was a campaign initiated by deaf students. DPN resulted in the replacement of a newly appointed hearing president who had virtually no skills in sign language with Gallaudet's first deaf president.

In Canada, the "Deaf Ontario Now" (DON) movement of 1989 was inspired by the success of DPN at Gallaudet. As a result of DON's activities, Gary Malkowski became the first culturally deaf person in North America to be elected to a provincial or state legislature. In Toronto, York University appointed David Mason to the Faculty of Education. Mason, currently the director of York's program to prepare teachers to work with students who are deaf and hard of hearing, is believed to be the first and only culturally deaf Canadian to have both earned a doctorate and be working in such a position in Canada.

When it comes to research, change has been much slower. This is especially true for the field of aural rehabilitation, my current area of interest. Aural rehabilitation is concerned with reducing the barriers to communication experienced by persons who are hard of hearing, that is, persons who use speech as their primary means of communication regardless of the degree of hearing loss. Most research in aural rehabilitation continues to be based on the positivist paradigm. Typical clinical practice, with its emphasis on diagnostic and prescriptive remediation, relies on the same outdated worldview within which treatment efficacy is narrowly defined as change in test scores.

What interests me about aural rehabilitation is the discrepancy between what persons who are hard of hearing say about aural rehabilitation classes and what test scores and results of quantitative research show. As an instructor in one of my studies said, "They tell you there's a difference; you can videotape them and see the difference, but the test scores say 'no difference.'"

When I began to do participant observation of aural rehabilitation classes, I observed hard-of-hearing persons who showed up for class on time, even in the worst weather; persons who eagerly engaged in group discussion and participated enthusiastically in all activities; persons who voluntarily repeated courses again and again to maintain friendships as well as skills.

In personal interviews, hard-of-hearing persons within these classes said they felt better about themselves; they were more self-confident and more willing to try to communicate in difficult listening situations, despite little if any change in scores on tests of speechreading or hearing handicap scales. One woman told me that classes made her feel alive; another said she had begun to take special care with her dress and makeup. A third explained, "All these hard-of-hearing people are staggering around in the dark. The course makes [us] feel like we can fight lions and tigers."

My research partner and I are increasingly conceptualizing the process of aural rehabilitation as a social construct. We are interested in exploring the different meanings that persons who are hard of hearing and significant others in their lives construct from the experience of hearing loss and its effect on communication and quality of life.

Sometimes there is agreement between the self-assessment of persons who are hard of hearing and the opinions of significant others. A woman with a progressive hearing loss, for example, believed she had made considerable gains during an intensive aural rehabilitation class. Instructors observing her progress concurred. Her husband said that the woman he married 35 years ago had been returned to him.

At other times there is disagreement, as in the case of a man with a severe hearing loss from birth who said, "I know what [a person who is hard of hearing] is supposed to do or at least what has been effective so far." Family members and former instructors, however, did not concur. From their perspective, this man still had a long way to go to become an effective communicator.

Interpretive/qualitative research, with its emphasis on reality as personal meaning-making, allows for these differences in perspective to be acknowledged and incorporated into a body of research that welcomes inconsistencies, as defined by traditional rationality, as part of the complexity of human experience.

The Ethics of Listening

I have come to believe that the field of aural rehabilitation can best be served by listening directly to the voices of persons who are hard of hearing and trying to understand the complexity of their lives as they are lived. "Listening," however, is not as easy or as innocuous as it sounds. Ethical issues have arisen for me as I attempt to sort out the nature of the researcher–participant relationship and my role as a researcher.

During interviews, for example, participants sometimes ask me for information and advice about issues related to hearing loss or the aural rehabilitation process. I am unsure whether to answer their questions, especially if they are insistent in their request. My uncertainty is perhaps because of the different and conflicting roles I take on: (1) my academic role as an interviewer who, according to traditional science, is supposed to remain neutral, (2) my maternalistic/feminine role as a nurturer and helper, (3) my professional role as a teacher and information provider, and (4) my recent conversion to seeing the researcher–interviewer relationship as a way of deepening knowledge and understanding without perpetuating inequality.

How do I make my way through the contradictory dimensions within myself? Frankly, I do not see a clear way. And looking back, there are situations I should have handled differently. But here and there, I come across a thought, an idea, or a different way of looking at things that helps me along. For instance, feminist researchers have begun to support the development of closer relations between interviewers and participants to minimize differences in status and promote participant involvement. When I read Andrea Fontana and James Frey's statement that "interviewers can show their human side and answer questions and express feelings" (Fontana & Frey, 1994, p. 370), I feel relieved and affirmed.

Yet such statements raise yet another set of issues. How can researchers "show their human side and answer questions and express feelings" (Fontana & Frey, 1994, p. 370) and "develop a sense of connectedness with people" (Reinharz, 1992, p. 20), while still maintaining an appropriate distance? Is there still such a thing as an appropriate distance? How can researchers ensure that the interview does not become a form of therapy? Where does one draw the line with regard to all these issues without reproducing paternalistic/patriarchal values and notions about the roles of researcher and participant? Is there still a line to draw?

Lous Heshusius's (1994) work on the participatory mode of consciousness has helped me begin to explore some possible responses to these questions. Heshusius explains that the researcher must "temporarily let go of all preoccupation with self and move into a state of complete attention" (p. 17) to what is observed and to the ideas and experiences that others want to share. Total attentiveness, however, does not guarantee a grasp of the participant's life. Rather, what is achieved is an absence, both of distance and of ego-centeredness. This stance, I think, satisfies the need for a coequal relationship and promotes a sense of connectedness.

Coequality and connectedness ask for participatory research, a form of action research in which researchers and the people being studied work as equal partners in planning and carrying out research designed to bring about individual and social change. I am currently involved in a participatory research project in collaboration with York University's Office for Persons With Disabilities and ABLE-York, a student advocacy group. We are developing a workshop on coping with hearing loss and a related qualitative research study. We have invited students who are deaf and hard of hearing to meet with a deaf facilitator to plan the workshop and to provide input into the data collection process for the research study. Our goals are to (1) understand the barriers at York that prevent students from maximizing their opportunities, and (2) help students become effective self-advocates. This project requires us to plan with rather than for prospective participants. Working through the process has challenged me to examine the vestiges of my patriarchal/paternalistic belief system and to try to relinquish all control. This has been much harder to do than I anticipated.

A source of help has been Reinharz (1992), who documents the work of feminists who have invented new ways to do research or have used old methods in novel ways. Two such methods that particularly appeal to me are group interview and self-interview techniques. Group interviews are useful for encouraging a flow of information and ideas. My first (and virtually only) question in a group interview study was, "Tell me what it's like to be hard of hearing." In response, there was an outpouring of stories, with people building on each other's experiences.

In a future study of hard-of-hearing persons who have attended aural rehabilitation classes, I hope to try out the self-interview technique, in which participants are invited to record their own thoughts and comments on audiotape. This approach will allow them to address issues of personal importance in the privacy of their own homes and over a longer period of time than a traditional personal interview would permit.

Reinharz (1992, pp. 214–239) reviews other research methods that may help people find their voices, incorporating the use of consciousness-raising groups, group diaries, dramatic role-plays, and photography.

Toward an Orthodoxy-Free Future

Harvard educator Eleanor Duckworth (1987) calls intellectual development "the having of wonderful ideas." She says there is nothing finer than raising a question for yourself and figuring out for yourself how to answer it.

The links between research and learning are obvious, for what is research if not raising questions and discovering or uncovering the answers in a process that is exciting, deepening, involving, and satisfying? But there is a limit to this analogy because it leaves out the collective side of research and theory-building. Duckworth's perspective, however, opens the door to the possibility of research as an "opportunity to wonder" (Melamed, 1985, p. 193). For me, this has been the allure of qualitative research—the chance "to organize ideas in new ways, to follow a truly emergent design and to move from what is to what might be" (Melamed, 1985, p. 193), in other words, to be free of the dogma associated with traditional research methods.

I have come to recognize, however, that the dangers of orthodoxy in research also exist within interpretive and qualitative methods. While analyzing one of my first sets of qualitative data, I myself fell prey to the need for orthodoxy. I wanted my data analysis to be a formulaic procedure, much like the computer-generated statistical analyses I had been accustomed to in my days of quantitative research. I was continually on the phone to a colleague, shrieking, "Data Emergency" to her answering machine in hopes that she would have mercy and pick up the phone to tell me which step to do next. Her typical response was, "Well, it depends . . . " I would keep asking the same question and she would keep giving the same answer (through clenched teeth, as time went on). It took me some time to realize that in qualitative research there should be no formulas.

In a similar vein, writing researcher Donald Graves (1984) critiqued the writing process movement in a piece entitled "The Enemy is Orthodoxy." He expressed concern about teachers' tendencies to view process writing as a series of explicitly defined steps that have to be followed in sequence. Graves did not wish to see process writing become so entrenched in dogma and conformity that it would lose the flexibility and creativity that have made it so beneficial. Orthodoxies, says Graves, "are substitutes for thinking. They clog our ears" (1984, p. 185). Future researchers will have to work hard to keep their ears unclogged and their orthodoxies at bay.

In the summer of 1994, education reporter William Honan said that in academia, professorial nastiness was at an all-time high. Will that still be the case in 2044? Or will there be a collegium of researchers engaged in collaborative, action-oriented, multidimensional, nonorthodox research? The cynic in me is doubtful.

I think of Honan's words again as he quotes Professor May:

Present day back-biting is mild compared with the invective that Leninists and Trotskyists flung at each other in the pages of *Partisan Review* in the 1930s. . . . Long before that academicians were known to have fought duels to settle their professional differences. (1994, p. 38)

With that past as our legacy, we have much work and much soul-searching to look forward to.

The Hunger for Wisdom

Mary Simpson Poplin

While growing up in Wichita Falls, Texas, I remember thinking it had to be the ugliest place on the earth. The trees were limited to scrubby mesquite, the land was flat and dry, and the weather extreme. But after I left and began to go back to see my family, I would find myself taking long drives outside of town with the windows open just to be with this land. One day my mother and I chased down the sunset for 50 miles and found a flock of scissortails as our reward. I remember the first time I read a novel by Larry McMurtry, a native of the same desolate countryside. His description of driving from one small town to the next in the heat of the summer was so accurate — the look of the road and the weeds alongside — that I felt I was there. As time has gone by, I notice that I prefer to schedule my airline connections in Dallas/Fort Worth, and when there is time I take the tram around the terminal just to look at the land and the sky. I long to feel and smell the air there in central Texas, and I go back as often as possible. I feel at home.

Such was the way I felt reading these stories. Like a good novel, they each reminded me of experiences, feelings, and thoughts I had had or could easily relate to. They caused me to feel connected to people I don't know. They made me feel less odd. The stories reveal the commonalities not only in our experiences but also in our searches, in our reasons for having "gone over to the other side." It seems we are all fleeing the smallness, yearning to connect, longing to find wisdom, and seeking to know things we felt we could sense but not come to understand when burdened with the rules of narrow methods. We want to stretch ourselves out and know with our total beings. To the extent we allow ourselves to do so, how can we encourage those we teach to do the same?

Certainly the methods of qualitative, interpretive research have made us feel more connected. As Curt Dudley-Marling suggests, this way of being in research connects who we are in private with who we are in public, the personal and the professional. Qualitative research, while much more difficult to do well, yields much more understandable and complete descriptions of experience. These descriptions allow us and others to fluidly partake in the picture that is painted as life versus contorting ourselves to fit into those complicated labyrinths of logical machinations which, once completed, felt wholly inadequate. Research in the social "sciences" should make us feel more human. If our own story as a human being is not there in our pages, the research cannot be true, yet if it is *only* our story, it is also not true. This paradox should be laid open in the richness of the dialectic, so that we do not lose the richness and the diversity of the world. That is part of the joy and the rigor of interpretive research.

I remember being on an airplane about a year ago with a man who was in the window seat, I in the aisle seat. We were flying from Southern California to Dallas/Fort Worth as he looked outside over Arizona and remarked that there was nothing out there to see. I didn't say anything, but it made me think hard about what it is to see and not see. I wondered and wonder how much I still don't see. Our stories tell the tales of tearing off the blinders that traditional research methods put in part of our eyes. Traditional methods have long dulled our senses, occluded our vision methodologically. Deborah Gallagher and Neita Israelite question the role of method in both research and teaching. I believe they are right. Our teaching methods also inhibit growth rather than promote it, just as the research methods that stemmed from the same reductionistic philosophies inhibited our vision or the admission of our vision. Perhaps we have come further in the university in lifting the blinders on research than we have on teaching. In teaching we are more directly vulnerable, we are the watched.

Is there a proper place for quantitative methods? When should we use them? How might we pool our gifts with those who use other methods (historical, philosophical, artistic) to better research issues of human life? How might we as teachers of qualitative inquiry help our students find their own gifts and develop the insight necessary for such inquiry?

We should be careful to continue to question our own methods of qualitative research as well. How much do we still limit our vision in qualitative inquiry? How much of our "data" are not allowed to see the light? How much do we not see either? How much do we still limit our "data" by the questions we ask, the way we observe and analyze, who we are? Would it not be best to engage in qualitative research with diverse teams who can contribute multiple meanings to multiple texts of life to find truths within the story of our collective lives? Do our methods still help us gain worldly knowledge and lose wisdom? How do we sort out what is from what should be? How do our methods encourage social action versus merely knowing? How does our method favor — or not favor — differences, uniqueness? How often do our own interpretations cleanse and generalize through abstraction? These questions trouble me because I fall into their trap.

Our stories reveal a primary reason we are attracted to qualitative research: a longing to be with the larger issues of life. I am reminded of Sigmund Koch's address to the American Psychological Association in 1981, in which he mourned the separation of psychology from philosophy that created a reductionistic "science" that could no longer even admit interest in issues such as the meaning of life. Yet it is these larger issues of meaning that fill our stories as they fill everyone's life. In our own stories we freely use religious metaphors, such as Egon Guba's road to Damascus, Lous Heshusius's call for us to do our work in the context of high spirits, and Tom Schwandt's fear of loss of spirit. Page Smith, in his critical book on higher education, *Killing the Spirit* (1990), points out that one of the original purposes of colleges and universities was to merge "the hearing of God's word with the doing." It was to be the ideal blending of the religious and the scientific life. We were not only to study and report, we were to study and act.

In our "Voices" study inside schools (Poplin & Weeres, 1992), children's and adolescents' primary complaint about the pedagogy they receive in schools was the absence of people who would raise issues or allow them to raise issues of the "really important things in life." In their descriptions of aspects of school they like, they describe teachers (not subjects or classes) that raise issues of life, teachers who share their deepest thoughts with their students and encourage them to do the same. But we also found that teachers were often afraid to raise important issues with children, such as racism or religion. Students have no qualms about either of these; their texts and their interviews are filled with things adults feel uncomfortable discussing. One middle school child says: "If they want us to make a better world, they have to talk inside the school." Another said, "It's fun to talk about God with my friends."

Even more estranged from our public, professional discourse than our personal lives are our religious and spiritual lives. How does my being a Christian affect the meanings I make, the things I see, the things I care about, and the issues in my own life that are, of course, not separate from my work? How does reading the Koran influence the child in Curt Dudley-Marling's class? Why did some of the students in our study (Poplin & Weeres, 1992) believe that the most important thing about school was a Levite Club that met before school for prayer and on Fridays after school? How is it that this group of youngsters, who meet early on campus to pray, defined for themselves the goal of helping kids who hate school to like it? What a paradox that their energy goes to promote a system that cannot recognize their club.

Perspective is the most critical issue in interpretive work. So often we are in the position of interpreting the meanings of those whose experience is very different from ours. The experience with the "Voices" project also brought this home to me. There we used participatory research to an extent not often practiced. The data collection was designed and drawn from all the players at four schools—the students, teachers, parents, staff members, and administrators. For the interpretation of major themes, we have a multiethnic research team drawn from those who worked in various positions (from staff to professional administrators and teachers). I cannot overstate the importance that the interpretive team be diverse, especially in the ethnic and class or status differences. Issues were revealed that few of us would have seen or known otherwise. For example, because of the high concentration of teachers and university faculty who were Euro-American (which was the reverse of the staff and student body), the issue of racism could easily have been perceived as an issue of poor relationships. In fact, this difference in perspective continues to be a struggle, as the following incident illustrates.

After attending the unveiling of the report, a local newspaper reporter wrote a caption for a picture that stated that multiethnic children were hurt in schools by monocultural teachers. At the next meeting, a Euro-American member of the team hurled the paper to the middle of our table and said, "Can you believe he said this?" A Latina teacher picked up the paper and asked what was wrong; she saw nothing in the caption that shocked her. A long discussion, one of hundreds, ensued. Had there not been people of color on the team, there would have been considerable energy expended to cover up or rename the issues of racism raised by students.

John Rivera (1992), an American Council on Education Research fellow with the project that year, noted in his essay that Rodney King, the Simi Valley jurors, and the Los Angeles police have one thing in common. They are educated by the same system. How is it, then, that we pay so little attention to multiple perspectives and interpretations in our research? Wouldn't our interpretations be so much richer if we were to involve multiethnic teams of interpreters? How can we come to any truths when we leave out large percentages of people from doing the analysis (even though they occupy large percentages of our world)? Herein lie issues of validity barely touched. They are more than issues of validity. They are issues of who gets to name experiences that go far beyond typical research agendas. We so often underestimate the power we have to name.

To draw out the voices of those not accustomed to being asked or heard, there must be extraordinary efforts to create safe spaces to talk in which particular groups are not seen as a minority. I believe our methods need to concentrate on this meaning of validity. Will we allow ourselves these checks on our methods and our interpretations, these places to listen and to learn? We have all experienced our own and another's silence when sensitive issues are spoken about and we know the agony of it. John Smith in this volume expresses a similar sentiment with regard to gender. I believe our inquiry will be richer, more wholesome if others (our research participants) are equally involved in our analysis and interpretations.

Then we could more adequately incorporate issues of the classic values of every culture and gender, the issues Tom Schwandt raises for us. If any branch of inquiry can study and act on values, it should be the interpretist. In our study of "Voices," we found the more we worked together across socioeconomic and ethnic boundaries, the more we could see the similarities of our values and our dreams for children and for education. We could also see the incredible difference in opportunities to express and actualize those values. Qualitative researchers must have not only the right methods but the civic courage it will take to work on issues of values, ethics, and morality. I believe the further we delve into these issues, the more likely it will be that our work contributes to the real transformations that are needed in society and in education.

The concentration on values, using multiple perspectives, might help us avoid the pitfalls of overintellectualizing or overemoting that so easily seep into interpretations and into teaching. In teaching and research our unconscious emotions and our overattention to the intellectual to the exclusion of other ways of knowing are passed on to our students. They will be the ones who pay for our sins, as it were.

Lous Heshusius reminds us to heighten our awareness to our bodies and to nature. The mind and heart receive information from all senses. We must create a way of being a researcher that encourages meanings to emerge from all our senses. And that will be difficult because so many of us live in our heads and, like Piaget, believe one knows only what one can tell with language. The more awake we are, the more alive will be our work. I believe our stories are a testimony to that.

The work of qualitative, interpretist inquiry is a moral task. It is composed of the intellectual, emotional, political, willful, cultural, social, and spiritual. It is much larger than ourselves and our professions. It is not really about amassing knowledge, it is about discerning wisdom. Therefore, it is beyond methodology. We talk about the wisdom to do something with our knowledge, but the deeper wisdom is the knowledge that the most important things in life are not the seen but the unseen or the hard to see.

In the 1500s, St. John of the Cross (Kavanaugh & Rodriguez, 1991) noted in his work on the dark night of the soul that the intellect must be darkened and tried by faith. This is wisdom, the unification of things seen and unseen. We often know wisdom when we see it, as in those who had the ability to see a man standing taller in Keith Ballard's story, or the wisdom Bill Rhodes seeks in the unification of art and science. As scholars, too, we must come closer to wisdom, to living it in our life and our work.

Coming Home

William C. Rhodes

In my reading of the stories of my fellow travelers and in experiencing, secondhand, the dark night of their souls as they gradually lost the true research faith, I anguished with them. Then, in the denouement, when they finally had a sense of "coming home," as Keith Ballard puts it, I, too, experienced his "sense of relief," his "sense of harmony" in "how he thought about the world through research." With the exception of one — maybe two — stories, this is what I experienced in my reading of the rest. It was like coming home over and over for me.

This "dark-night-of-the-soul" experience is not exactly a religious experience, but it tends in that direction. When Keith Ballard said he had the experience of coming home, I seemed to remember an old hymn by that name.

Many of the others also experienced actual persecution at the hands of their colleagues. Is that the openness of scholarship? Thomas Schwandt expresses it most vividly. He reports that he often encountered situations in which colleagues would ask him to defend interpretive work and what he was about, as if he were appearing before the Spanish Inquisition. He began to realize, he said, that many of these encounters were not simply (or even) about matters of epistemology. They were about the politics of method. When he said this, I remembered Thomas Kuhn's (1970) discussion of the politics of scientific revolutions. Schwandt then goes on to say he realized that an orthodoxy was in place, and he was throwing stones at the Temple.

I thought to myself over and over as I read one story after the other, "Damn, these are good writers — every living soul of them. How could they help from becoming interpretivists, being such good interpreters of their own lives — their own life-worlds." I wondered if it was necessary to be a good writer to be an interpretivist. It might be easier for people without this expressive facility to try to share their perceptions of reality through numbers.

In reading these accounts of change, I asked myself how these writers managed to summon the courage to defect from the dominant group consensus, especially a consensus so heavily institutionalized in the scholarly community. Are they naturally rebels, or are they very strong people? In considering this, I had to examine my own motivational system, my own makeup. My answer for myself was, Yes, I must be a rebel. Much of my life attests to that. But how did I prevent myself from being excommunicated or institutionalized? And then I thought, How did these writers and researchers escape the same fate?

Many of these researchers must have gone through the experience of being othered, being made different. I know that I did. Although none of us were burned at the stake, I'm sure we all felt the heat of the fire.

In reading my fellow travelers' accounts of their journey from positivism to interpretivism, I am impressed with the fact that in the transition, many of us were very conscious of our own self-doubts and our sense of gradual alienation from our own professional strengths. In many of the cases, my fellow writers speak of a growing aversion to a point of view that was alien to their own value and belief systems. I can certainly relate to that. It is amazing how successfully we adapted, propounded, and advanced our careers in spite of our divided selves. All of us seem to have had successful careers. Did success make it possible to come out of the closet?

There seems to be a theme of moral concern running throughout our stories. All of us seem to have had trouble in the area of morality, but perhaps that goes with the territory of self-introspection and self-doubt. Are morally preoccupied people self-doubters, and more introspective? At the opposite end, however, do all of these researchers have to fight the sense of moral superiority I sometimes fight in myself? Or, perhaps, is it that our colleagues accuse us of claiming moral superiority?

The young, or interpretivists of the future, who do not have to shed their positivist skins, will probably not have to go through the "conversion experience," but surely they will see the lack of moral depth in the old Newtonian science.

Although many of us seem to recall clearly defining moments—a professional confrontation, a vivid moment of awareness of repressed doubts, a hot bath, a classroom event, a particular book, a particular lecture, and so forth—in every case, the conversion experience seems to be very gradual, sometimes even a return to the roots of childhood.

Mary Poplin says, "I have a deep sense that my transition as an adult has in some significant ways been a trip back to things I knew as a child (perhaps not consciously) and lost along the way." Keith Ballard says, "I well recall the day I was introduced to Skinner and animal training. My reaction was one of disbelief and a sense of anger." Lous Heshusius was even more repulsed, as she tells of her first class in graduate school in the United States. She was half an hour late when she found the class, where the professor was discussing ratology. She was horrified, and then stunned when she discovered he was speaking about the behavior of laboratory rats in the same field of education where she had been influenced by Montessori's and Piaget's research and theories of child development. For her, as distinguished from the other contributors to this book, it was a profound cultural shock.

In contrasting this reaction and that of Keith Ballard in his account of his reaction to animal training, my own background of training and experience found animal experiments fascinating in clinical psychiatry and psychology. I was excited that animal-type experiments could mimic or even reproduce human "neuroses" and then "cure" them. It seemed to make learning theory a very heuristic model in the education and reeducation of emotionally disturbed children.

Guba tells us that for him the conversion process was labored, and not at all appreciated during the time that it was taking place. Like others, he reports that the process was visceral rather than rational. John Smith talks about having gone through a long, dry period of seven years when he did not write or publish anything, a period during which he could only occasionally force himself to read quantitative studies.

My own visceral reactions to positivist science did not reveal themselves to me until I heard Lous Heshusius describe her physical revulsion to ratology. I had been one of those animal psychologists. I was not aware of the past physical part of my negative reactions to positivism until she talked to me about that experience.

What I do remember, however, was an almost physical reaction of avoidance of quantitative research that increased gradually in me over the course of the early to late 1970s. In the way that John Smith talks about splitting himself in two as his revulsion grew, he describes what I deliberately did to myself in the early days of moving from writer to classic scientist. Much later, in becoming a proponent of the "new science," the non-Newtonian science, I returned to my roots as an interpretivist, a follower of the humanities, and a postrevolutionary or postmodern scientist.

Something that is clear as I read through these accounts is the interlocking of professional and personal journey portrayed here. Perhaps if we had been able to keep these two areas of our lives separate in watertight compartments, we would never have changed. On the other hand, we might have become even more disturbed. Along with this is the seeming need for authenticity displayed here. Perhaps it was the melding of the personal and professional that was the reason for transformation. But maybe every creative scientist and researcher experiences this. In the last chapter of *The Day the Universe Changed*, James Burke (1985) talks about Einstein and the great conceptual leap that changed physics, and with it the fundamental nature of matter and the way the universe worked:

> . . . he said it came to him as if in a dream. He saw himself riding on a beam of light and concluded that if he were to do so, light would appear to be static. (p. 303)

Burke then talks about other great eruptions of the personal into the professional. August Kekule, the discoverer of the benzine ring, wrote of gazing into the fire and seeing a ring of atoms like a serpent eating its own tail. Wallace came to the theory of evolution in a "delirium" (Burke, 1985, p. 303).

These wondrous personal eruptions remind me of Guba's "little green man who inhabits a securely locked room somewhere in my head."

One of the things that has amazed me, and that I resonate to, as I read these accounts was the extent to which some of these interpretivists took confrontation and ridicule—took dross, and in my mind, turned it into gold. As, for example, in Egon Guba's case, who was almost laughed off the podium when he presented his first qualitative evaluation at a U.S. Office of Education conference. He was later accused by a colleague of introducing a major schism in the profession.

Some contributors talk about their anxiety about leading students down the garden path, encouraging them to become interpretivists at the same time that they themselves were being ridiculed and vilified. I have certainly had that concern. However, I, like Guba, have a "little green man" locked inside my head. He has been there all along as I traveled my own personal journey.

I was aware of my little green man's presence way back when I began my career as a writer, constantly surprising me with his messages from beyond. I have learned to depend on him for my own enrichment, my own movement from where I was to where I am going. As distant and mysterious as he is, I know he is part of me, perhaps the core of me.

I don't think he is socialized, because he keeps getting me into trouble, even though I myself am socialized. Sometimes I despair of him, but I have never wanted to get rid of him. For he has far greater wisdom than I do—

Right there! He just gave me a message. "Wisdom!" That's it. The Old Testament wisdom! That's it—the "divine Spirit." Shades of Carl

Jung: It isn't even a "he." It is a "she," my complementary side. I search out Jung's (1933) book, *Modern Man in Search of a Soul*, and read him:

> The living spirit grows and even outgrows its earlier form of expression—This living spirit is eternally renewed and pursues its goals in manifold and inconceivable ways throughout the history of mankind. Measured against it, the names and forms which men give it means little enough; they are only the changing leaves and blossom on the stem of the eternal tree. (p. 244)

New Songs of Innocence and Experience? (With Apologies to William Blake)

Thomas A. Schwandt

A few years ago I had the opportunity to give a series of lectures on qualitative, responsive approaches to program evaluation at the Lilly Endowment. The audience was composed of Endowment staff from its religion, community service, and education divisions, along with a variety of contract evaluators whom the Endowment often called upon to help evaluate its programs.

In the lectures I talked about the importance of case study as a means of illuminating the ways in which program staff and participants experienced a program and made meaning of their experiences. Following the lead of work by Bruner (1985, 1987), Coles (1989), Grumet (1991), Polkinghorne (1988), and others, I explored the idea of narrative as a way of knowing and talked about how we might link narrative as both inquiry and text to doing and reporting program evaluations. We also explored evaluation as a means of learning about programs and their participants and contrasted that with evaluation as a technology for improving decisionmaking. The general theme of the lectures was that thinking of evaluation as a socioanthropological, interpretive undertaking would be more edifying, informative, and, ultimately, useful than thinking of it as a science of measurement and assessment best employed as handmaiden to program administrators.

During and after the lectures I was greeted by two very distinct kinds of reactions. Audience members with backgrounds in the humanities generally smiled and nodded approvingly during the lectures. They often mentioned works in their fields that they thought reflected this kind of understanding of evaluating as a way of interpreting ourselves to ourselves. Afterward they would ask me why I talked as if this interpretive, socioanthropological approach to understanding was so different and radical. In effect, they were saying to me, "What's the big deal?" Audience members with backgrounds in educational, clinical, and organizational psychology or training as sociologists had a very different reaction. They quizzed me throughout the lectures. They challenged the lack of certainty in an interpretive approach to evaluation; they expressed fear that it lacked validity and reliability and was nothing more than the personal opinions of program participants, or worse, of the evaluator. They wanted me to explain in detail the methods one would use to conduct this kind of evaluation; they wanted to know what textbooks I might recommend that explained this kind of approach.

When I finished reading the stories in this volume, this experience immediately came to mind. As teacher-scholars we are socialized to see the world in particular ways, to adopt particular theoretical perspectives, to find problems of a certain kind worthy of explanation, to employ particular means for investigating those problems, and so forth. In short, we learn to become a member of a tribe with its own rites and ceremonies and worldviews. Other tribes with other worldviews seem alien to us.

It is a truism (and some would say, a tragedy) that the modern social sciences have looked to the natural sciences and not the humanities for ideas about their purpose, method, and use. It is also a truism that in some social scientific undertakings, most notably psychology, naturalistic ideals have their strongest appeal. Although there have been challenges from within to the belief that the psychological sciences should be modeled on the natural sciences (e.g., humanistic or third force psychology, ecological psychology, debates over statistical significance testing, and, more recently, narrative psychology and social constructionism), a set of ideas about what constitutes legitimate social scientific inquiry has survived. These ideas include isolating questions of fact from possible contamination by questions of meaning; using a specialized language to test and express knowledge claims; separating the knower as much as possible from the object of her or his inquiry so as to prevent the intrusion of inquirer bias; and rejecting the idea that understanding human action is different from understanding human behavior.

It is also generally recognized that the modern research university is characterized by a division between the sciences and the humanities and by increasing specialization within the sciences. Further, it is not news that the scientific paradigm of knowledge and its accompanying metaphors of objectivity, control, and utility exercise disproportionate and often exclusive influence on education. Seventy years ago, Whitehead (1953[1925]) noted that the 20th-century university is founded on a 17th-century scheme of scientific thought. Finally, most of us realize that the university is a place that embodies the Cartesian partitioning of mind and body; it is a place where the self is recognized more for its technical and professional abilities and less for its performance of traditional ways and rituals (Wilshire, 1990). It is a place where reason prevails, a place where we have generally forgotten Dewey's advice that human beings are thinkers only in the second instance. In the first instance, the self is an agent-patient, doer, sufferer, and enjoyer (Dewey, 1929; Westbrook, 1991). Broadening the empirical field to include participatory knowledge and thinking through the body (e.g., Jackson, 1989) is not easily done in academe. The university is a place that teaches students that they learn by accumulating tested propositions about the objective world, not by participating in social practices, by assuming social roles, or by becoming familiar with exemplary narratives and the lives of typical characters who illustrate a variety of patterns of human action (Bellah et al., 1991).

And so it is not all that surprising that a central theme echoes throughout many of the stories here—a voice that has been "shut off from ordinary human learning and experiences"; a voice unable "to ask the questions which were of interest to me"; a voice speaking of a lack of "harmony between how I learned about the world personally, in everyday life, and how I thought about the world through research"; a voice "relieved and vindicated" on learning that there was another way of knowing about the world, and so on.

The stories in this book are stories of being socialized to the tribe of the psychologist and the larger tribe of the professional scholar—both cultures of impersonal inquiry. Socialization meant learning to set aside a personal self in order to adopt the mantle of the scientific self; to use methods of data collection and analysis that promised precision but sacrificed involvement; to treat the social world as a world of facts "out there" waiting to be discovered. As a similar tale of a personal journey in academe revealed (Reinharz, 1979), somewhere during the process of becoming socialized to this world or after having been awarded full membership in the tribe, many of us experienced something that led us to imagine that there might be another culture, another tribe, that saw the world differently. Often gradually, but sometimes suddenly, like Saul of Tarsus on the road to Damascus, we began to learn about these other ways of knowing and being.

In many ways, the stories of these discoveries echo the Romanticist reaction to the Enlightenment. They celebrate the personal, the subjective, the emotional, and the imaginative in the face of a culture of social scientific inquiry that values and celebrates the power of reason and the intellect, the suppression of self, adherence to procedure, and so on. I am reminded of one of the great English Romantic poets, William Blake,

whose poems expressed, in part, his rejection of the intellectual orientation of the Enlightenment and the wretched material and spiritual condition of humanity in England in the late 18th century (Frye, 1966). Our
current situation may not be so wretched, but Blake's *Songs of Innocence
and of Experience* (subtitled "Shewing the Two Contrary States of the
Human Soul") is a particularly illuminative metaphor for envisioning
two different worlds.

Suppose we were to view the stories in this volume as *fin de siècle*
songs of innocence and experience, as poetry of the 20th-century social
inquirer reflecting upon her or his world. Songs of innocence for the
inquirer express a naive understanding of a social world and of an inquirer who can gaze upon that world with detachment and without fear
of involvement. These songs celebrate the rational, the objective, the
planned. They tell of how we have neatly solved epistemological (and
moral) questions. Songs of experience are not necessarily dark and fore-
boding (as are Blake's), but they are dramatically different. They tell of
how knowing the world in which we live is a lot more complex undertaking than we once thought. They celebrate the reunion of intellect and
passion, cognition and emotion, that we discarded several centuries ago;
they reveal how where we stand in looking at our world has something
to do with what we see. They celebrate knowing in relationship and all
the problems that entails.

We are part of a moment in human inquiry when many songs of
experience are being heard. Some of these songs relate struggles with
subjectivity and emotions in developing accounts of respondents' lived
experience (Ellis & Flaherty, 1992; Krieger, 1991). Some are about the
bricolage that now characterizes a diverse set of purposes and methods
in interpretive inquiry (Denzin & Lincoln, 1994b). As suggested by the
stories in Chapter 2 of this volume, many of these songs are about
personal narrative and story now rising to a place of importance once
occupied solely by the well-formed argument. We are coming to realize
the power of rhetoric and of narrative and dialogue for understanding
ourselves and others. Of course, this is something that poets and novelists have long recognized but that social scientists are only now discovering (Geertz, 1988; Hunter, 1990; Rushdie, 1990).

As social inquirers and as teachers of other social inquirers, we have
a special obligation to put the use of stories to good service in our bid to
understand ourselves and others. We must be careful not to consider the
telling of songs of experience an end in itself. Just how we can avoid this
is not all that clear to me at present, although there are at least two
interesting directions along which to look. One is suggested by Walker's
(1992) explanation of an alternative moral epistemology that arises from

feminist ethics. She observes that the characteristic emphasis of feminist ethics on personal relations, attunement to particular persons and contexts, emotional responsiveness, and narrative knowing comprises a different set of expectations about what it means to be in the world in relation to others.

Walker's primary concern is with what this means for our conception of moral agents and our understanding of moral reasoning, yet I find her ideas proactive for rethinking our understanding of the obligations of the social inquirer and the purpose of social inquiry. Walker's notion of an alternative moral epistemology suggests at least two ideas: First, that understanding the life experiences of others must take into account the normative claim that others' lifeways make upon the inquirer; this means, as Nussbaum (1990) observes, having the willingness and capacity to be touched by another's life. Second, knowledge *of* the other is always interactional and best characterized in terms of moral notions (e.g., reception, recognition, obligation), not simply procedural and descriptive terms. In other words, knowing the other is not a quiescent capacity resident only in the person of the inquirer but a shared undertaking, a relationship, with moral dimensions.

We continue to explore these ideas in practice in our work here at Indiana. Three recent efforts include the studies undertaken by Leslie Bloom, now at Iowa State University, Peter Magolda, now at Miami University (Ohio), and James Arnold. Bloom's (1993) dissertation, *"Shot Through with Streams of Songs": Explorations of Interpretive Research Methodology*, explored the notion of nonunitary subjectivity and experimented with textual representation of her own and her respondents' narratives in order to display this kind of subjectivity. Magolda (1994) not only built his work around respondents' stories but explored the ethics and politics of his interpersonal relationships with respondents in his dissertation, *A Quest for Community: An Ethnographic Study of a Residential Community College*. And James Arnold (1995) grounded his dissertation, *Alcohol and the Chosen Few: Organizational Reproduction in an Addictive System*, in his biography and experimented in the text with the presentation of self and subjectivity intermingled with the life experiences of his respondents and his interpretations of same.

Another related and promising way of reuniting cognitive and emotional capacities in the service of social inquiry is suggested by Noddings's (1991) efforts to view narrative, dialogue, and stories as ways in which we engage in interpersonal reasoning. She borrows a definition from Norma Haan, who describes interpersonal reasoning as involving "moral dialogue between agents who strive to achieve balanced agreement, based on compromise they reach or on their joint discovery of interests they hold in common" (quoted in Noddings, 1991, p. 158). Noddings explains that this kind of reasoning stands in sharp contrast to "logico-mathematical reasoning that proceeds step by step according to a priori rules." Interpersonal reasoning, in Noddings's view, is "open, flexible, and responsive. It is guided by an attitude that values the *relationship* of the reasoners over any particular outcome, and it is marked by attachment and connection rather than separation and dialogue" [emphasis added] (p. 158).

What this means for the practice of social and educational research is that our endless focus on achievement goals and behavioral outcomes and the incredible proliferation of sophisticated measurement schemes are all part of the problem. None of this research is in any significant way *for* the people we study, it is only *about* them. Noddings has some suggestions here, too. She recommends "fidelity to persons" in educational research that, in turn, "counsels us to choose our problems in such a way that the knowledge gained will promote individual growth and maintain the caring community. It is not clear that we are sufficiently concerned with either criterion at present" (Noddings, 1986, p. 506). She argues that research *for* educators would be concerned with the actual needs, views, and experiences of teachers and administrators rather than focus on the outcomes produced through various educational innovations in curriculum, classroom management, school structure, and the like (Noddings, 1988).

The telling of stories, or songs of experience if you will, signals the return of the inquirer as a morally and emotionally engaged knower. As social inquirers, we are obligated to explore how acknowledging and celebrating this engagement furthers our efforts to interpret ourselves to ourselves. We cannot simply repudiate reason and the intellect in favor of passion and the emotions. We must find ways of bringing both to bear simultaneously in our social practice as inquirers. This cannot be achieved by means of some new formula or research design; it is not principally a matter of new procedures but of a different way of understanding our being in the world.

An Opportunity Lost?

John K. Smith

At the time (summer 1994) that I am writing about what I would wish the future of educational research to be like, it has been about two years since I have written much of interest or consequence. Other than my story in the first part of this book, the last paper I wrote was entitled "The Stories Educational Researchers Tell About Themselves." This paper was presented at the Annual Meeting of the American Educational Research Association in 1992, but I have not yet put it in shape for possible publication. After approximately 10 years of writing with intensity about the nature of inquiry, especially interpretive inquiry, I have reached a lull. I seem to have said all I am presently capable of saying about the nature of inquiry. It will be interesting to me to see whether this lull is a temporary or lengthy one. I do not know on what it will depend.

In any event, how have I occupied my time over the last two years? Mostly by doing the things normally done in this profession — teaching undergraduates, working with doctoral students, attempting to avoid committee meetings, and reading. On various occasions, however, I have thought about what has and has not happened in the world of educational research since the early 1980s, when qualitative inquiry began to receive greater acceptance from educational researchers.

There can be no doubt that the contributors to this volume, among many others, have had an impact on the educational research community as a result of their writings, presentations, and teachings. The tangible evidence for this impact is abundant. Almost all of the introductory educational research textbooks now have at least one chapter devoted to qualitative inquiry, it seems like almost everyone fancies herself/himself as a qualitative researcher, many researchers — even long-time empiricists — now seem obliged to at least say that they have "analyzed" their data both quantitatively and qualitatively, and the criticisms of this approach to inquiry have been greatly tempered (at least in public).

Over the last two years I have pondered what this rapid and apparently general acceptance of qualitative inquiry means for the future of educational research. I am of two minds on this point. On the one hand, my optimistic side says that this acceptance is a stage in a general transition among educational researchers toward thinking of our world as constructed or made rather than found or discovered. If so, then we are on our way to a profound reconceptualization of who we are and what we do as researchers. On the other hand, my pessimistic side says that this acceptance means that qualitative inquiry has been "co-opted" and that the realization that social reality is made rather than found has been effectively blunted. And if this is the case, then an opportunity for fundamental change has been, if not lost, certainly seriously delayed.

At the moment, I think my pessimistic side is offering the most appropriate interpretation of what is happening and has happened with the qualitative movement in educational research. As I look over our research textbooks, for example, it is clear to me that there has been a strong movement to systematize qualitative inquiry and, in the process, tame it. Put differently, I fear that far too many educational researchers have come to think of the qualitative approach as little more than an additional set of research procedures or techniques that are to be employed in the name of that unrealizable empiricist goal of the discovery, as it actually is, of an independently existing reality.

The problem is that the ideas that led to the demise of empiricism and the advance of interpretive perspectives, such as the collapse of the subject–object and fact–value distinctions and the realization that there can be no theory-free observation, have been contained. The force of these ideas has had very little impact on most educational researchers and, as a result, on the accompanying crucial realization that we must see reality as something we make rather than discover. I can think of no better evidence of this situation than the fact that many who call themselves qualitative researchers continue to describe their work and themselves in terms of discovery(ers) and finding(ers) rather than in terms of constructing(ers) and making(ers).

This limiting of qualitative inquiry to an alternative set of methodic practices was directly a result of the lack of interest on the part of most researchers in the discussions about the conceptual incompatibility of the quantitative and qualitative perspectives on inquiry. In 1986 I published an article with Lous (Smith & Heshusius, 1986) that, because of its early reception, I thought would prevent for some time to come a closing down of the conversation about the compatibility–incompatibility of these approaches and undermine the movement to turn qualitative inquiry into little more than a set of research techniques. I was overly optimistic, to say the least, because by 1990 or so the issues were decided in favor of the compatibilists. This happened not because they had the better arguments, but because educational researchers in general lost whatever interest they may have had in this discussion. I remember the editor of a major journal writing me to say that most researchers had become bored with philosophical discussions and were more interested in getting on with the task of doing their research.

Within this climate of a lack of interest in the conceptual and a desire to just get on with the task of doing research, various books of a "how to do qualitative inquiry" variety found very fertile ground. For example, a book by Miles and Huberman (1984) that attempted to standardize qualitative methods was very well received. The number of editions the book has gone through clearly attests to the fact that they struck a cord within the profession. Their message was quite clear: Researchers should leave the philosophical/epistemological issues to those who are most interested in them and get about the business of doing qualitative research—but do it properly. They detailed various procedures for doing qualitative inquiry, with the injunction to their colleagues that if you do not follow these procedures you will not do good research and if you do you will.

For many people—including the contributors to this volume—the technicians or proceduralists have entirely misunderstood the nature of qualitative inquiry. As can be seen in our stories in this volume, one of the most important things we have had to come to terms with in our transitions to interpretive inquiry is that there are no, and can be no, set of established procedures to ground this approach to inquiry. In fact, I might add that as qualitative research became increasingly proceduralized, many of us have avoided, to varying degrees, using that term because it no longer captures what we want to say about inquiry. This is why many of us either do not use the term or, at a minimum, mix "qualitative" with "interpretive" and "constructivist," and talk about "inquiry" rather than "research."

I have pondered over the last two years why things developed the way they did. The questions I have asked myself are on the order of, Why did not more people come to realize that the metaphors of discovery and finding must give way to the metaphors of making and constructing? Or, Why was the qualitative movement so easily coopted and reduced to an alternative method in the service of the impossible, to realize empiricist goals of prediction and control? A few possible, and related, reasons come to mind.

The first reason is reflected in my reading of the stories of the other contributors to this volume. The transitions seem to have what I might call an element of happenstance about them. That is, in one way or another, we all seem to have been in the right place at the right time. This is not to say that we did not have, from early on, a latent sense that something was wrong with the empiricist perspective on research. I suspect this sense was there in all of us from graduate school days and even before. Rather, it is to say that we were in a position where the latent could manifest itself — somatically initially, intellectually later.

Certainly this being in the right place at the right time is part of my story. I came to a university that favored good teaching and that did not place heavy demands on research productivity. I think it is very likely that had I gone to a research "factory" I would have gotten as caught up in turning out articles as anyone else. So I was able to act on my sense that quantitative inquiry was inadequate. I was able to turn out a few articles and then take off years from writing and research in order to read, think, and attempt to better understand why it felt wrong to me — all at very little personal risk. This does not imply that the other contributors to this volume were as free of personal risk as I was, only that I suspect they also found themselves, maybe without even necessarily knowing it, in a position where their sense that something was wrong could be attended to.

My point is that those of us who have acted on our somatic sense of who we are and how we felt it necessary to be as researchers are not special people morally, intellectually, or otherwise. I believe that the feeling that something is wrong with the standard form of research is felt much more generally than many believe. One difference is that we had a chance to act on this feeling, whereas many others have had to suppress it. The pressures of tenure, promotion, making a living, and so on — especially in the face of a tight job market over the last few years — should never be minimized.

But, this point granted, there is another twist that can be taken with regard to this idea of risk. I believe people still feel that there is a great deal of professional, and thereby personal, risk involved in embracing interpretive inquiry — at least the nonmethodic perspective on interpretive inquiry. This risk is not announced or discussed openly with any frequency, but nonetheless I believe it is felt, even if only in a nonarticulated sense, by many researchers. This risk plays itself out in various ways.

For one thing, there is always a risk involved if a person adopts a seriously unconventional position — one that is out of line with communally established ways of thinking about and doing something. In the case of educational research, someone who argues for a major break with established patterns and tells a different story about who we are and what we do is engaged in a very high-risk strategy. What I mean here is that if someone advances an unconventional way of thinking about and doing inquiry, one of two things is going to happen. If for some reason this break with convention is eventually accepted by other researchers, then the payoff for the innovator can be quite substantial in terms of recognition, prestige, and so on. However, and much more likely, if the break with what is normal and accepted is rejected or ignored, then the person is looking at the fate of being consigned to the wastelands of professional life.

I suspect there are researchers out there who have been attracted by different ways of thinking about and doing inquiry and have been intrigued by different metaphors to describe themselves and their work. But I also suspect that many of these people have weighed the risks, even if not consciously, and decided to take the safer route. The safer route, of course, is to stay fairly close to doing what is normal and accepted, but to advance one's career by attempting to do a little more of the normal and accepted than others are doing or maybe to do it a little better — whatever "better" might mean in any given case.

A further variation on this risk theme is related to the idea, mistaken though it may be, that there is a science of education and a technology of schooling. The point is that those who claim to be engaged in the practice of science very often make the further claim that others, such as laypersons and teachers, for example, should listen to them. After all, the whole idea behind the empiricist approach to inquiry was that researchers possessed a special method, based on a special methodology, that allowed them to get beyond the surface appearances. This, of course, is the source of the idea that research (scientific) knowledge can stand in judgment of common sense in the sense that when the two differ, the latter must give way to the former.

For those who have found comfort in this privileged claim to be heard, the nonmethodic understandings or interpretations offered by qualitative inquirers present a problem. As noted, one of the key realizations of the interpretive perspective is that there is no special method or set of procedures that allows researchers to penetrate appearances to discover how things really are. This inevitably means that researchers are as much engaged in making or constructing reality as they go along as is everyone else. The only difference is that researchers use different vocabularies to construct realities different from those constructed by parents, teachers, and so on.

If this is so, then it is easy to see why many educational researchers have approached interpretive inquiry cautiously and have attempted to tame and recast this perspective so as to bring it into service of the unobtainable, but nonetheless desired, empiricist and quantitative research goal of prediction and control. If researchers cannot claim that their work leads to prediction and control and a technology of schooling, then why should anyone pay special attention to them, give them grant money, and so on? For many researchers, to accept that inquiry is about telling more interesting stories about children, schooling, and so on is considered a massive retreat that must lead inevitably to a loss of status. Put differently, I think it is very difficult for many educational researchers to accept that our closest kin are in the humanities building, not the physics building.

One final turn of this risk theme. The transition to an interpretive stance is very difficult because it means adopting a new way of thinking about everything—who we are and how we act as researchers, our relationships to other people, and so on. As was evident in the stories in Chapter 2, to reject quantitative inquiry is, in effect, to reject hundreds of years of established Western modes of thought. To one degree or another, anyone raised in the West is a child of the Enlightenment, with the corresponding emphasis on a particular style of intellectual reasoning, a particular definition of rationality, and so on. How does one give up on something that so deeply permeates our ways of thinking—both professionally and in our daily lives? The stories in this book all reflect, if nothing else, how much time and effort went into the transition we all experienced.

Thus my pessimistic side leads me to believe, for the moment anyway, that what has been so rapidly accepted is a very sanitized or tamed version of qualitative inquiry. This means that an opportunity has been lost. Richard Rorty once said that not much turns on the issue of whether we adopt the imagery of the world as one we discover as opposed to one we make. While I initially thought he was correct in this statement, I no longer do. Lawrence Hazelrigg (1989) has easily convinced me that a great deal turns on this distinction and the realization of what it means to use the metaphors of made or constructed versus those of discovered or found.

My point is that if we truly understand that as researchers we construct realities, we are obligated to further understand that we are responsible—morally so—for what we have constructed. The problem with the empiricist/quantitative perspective, with its subject–object dichotomy, fact–value split, and metaphors of discovery and finding, is that it separates us from ourselves. This perspective has left us with the fiction that somehow we can have separate perceptions of what is and of what ought to be and, as such, the moral is allowed to remain as a contingent category in the minds of researchers. The interpretive perspective dispenses with these false dichotomies and forces us to realize that the moral goes to the very center of our beings.

What will happen to educational research and educational researchers over the next few decades is, of course, impossible to say with certainty. Will the interpretive movement remain blunted? This could happen, because the transition to the interpretive perspective involves a very difficult break with the past. However, it is also possible that in the longer term educational research will be radically reshaped. It is apparent that there are pockets of people, like the contributors to this volume, who are using a different vocabulary and different metaphors; they are telling different stories about research and researchers. These groups— under whatever labels they now congregate—may continue to grow in numbers and influence and, thereby, increasingly reshape our thinking. I hope so, because if this is the case, then it will be all for the good. Then we will cease to do the kind of research that not only separates us from other people, but also separates us from ourselves. We will no longer do the kind of research that allows us to avoid responsibility for the choices we make and the worlds we construct.

4

Afterthoughts

Lous Heshusius and Keith Ballard

Very little in our language or culture encourages looking at
others as parts of ourselves.
                                        Patricia Williams (1991, p. 62)

I am interested in what prompts and makes possible this
process of entering what one is estranged from . . .
                                        Toni Morrison (1992, p. 4)

Just as we started to think of what we still wanted to say in our closing
comments, a colleague gave us a cartoon, portraying René Descartes's
gravestone, above which it says: "I thought, therefore I was." Whatever
the cartoonist wanted to express by humoring the legacy of Descartes,
we thought instantly of this book! The idea that thought equals existence, and that we can, and indeed have to, think ourselves out of difficulties, is at the core of many human problems. With Descartes the idea
of the fully substantial autonomous self was born, a self fundamentally
separate from everything, most of all from its own body. Now that we
have started to understand the ideological values that informed the view
of a purely thinking self, we can more consciously and deliberately live
and work differently. For we cannot continue to work in a disembodied
way and yet expect to understand life in an embodied way; that would
be making another journey in the mind only, perpetuating the same core
problem. How we actually live, feel, and know are inseparable. The
stories in Chapter 2 illustrate that correcting for the suppression of somatic and emotive knowing is not a matter of "stirring a little feeling into

existing forms of scientific . . . theorizing," to borrow a phrase from Jagger and Bordo (1989, p. 7), but rather necessitates "a radical revisioning of the prevailing opposition between emotions and thought."

This work, then, claims no more (but no less) than having provided accounts of how a particular source of knowing has been devalued, denied, and repressed in social and educational research. The paradigm shift from positivist to interpretivist thought provided the means by which we could illustrate the significance of the somatic and the emotive in the construction of formal knowledge.

There are, of course, limits to what the explicit welcoming of somatic-emotive knowing can contribute. We are not suggesting that explicit attentiveness to somatic-emotive sources will automatically confer sensitivity to social and ecological contexts and needs. The impulses for such sensitivity can be many. As these stories show, however, *what* we do with inner life can be instrumental in putting one "in touch" or "out of touch" with social inequities, with doubt, and with sensitivities beyond the self. In our tales, somatic-emotive life appears to function as a mediating force between a self that had been defined as an individual, rational thinker on the one hand, and a self that is inseparable from community and from the construction of knowledge of the other. Concerns regarding the ethics, the power inequalities, and the methodological complexities that emerge when it is acknowledged that the researcher is embedded in the very issues he or she addresses are extensively discussed and theorized in the literature. What the present stories illuminate is the intimate relationship between inner life and these larger social and ethical issues. Their many-layered interaction is mediated by somatic-emotive knowing as much as by rational analysis.

At the same time, inner life is only one source that mediates between the idea of the self-enclosed individual and the individual as part of other. Knowledge also issues, of course, from external sources (from history and herstory, and from cultural, social, and political structures, policies, and conflicts), often in ways that no longer reflect the somatic-emotive motives that were initially involved. We see the significance of the present stories, then, as adding to, rather than replacing, other accounts of the relationship between individual and social selves in knowledge construction. The ever-deepening questions of justice, power, and the quality of life, and the issue of who gets to name and ask these questions, make appeals well beyond reference to somatic-emotive life; but they should not exclude an explicit recognition of these important sources of primary information.

Acknowledging the significance of the somatic and the emotive does not remove doubt or uncertainty. Rather, this acknowledgment puts us deeper in touch with life as uncertainty. When emotive and somatic life were repressed to let reason and rationality reign, human reasoning was propelled into overdrive, rallying toward certainty in ways that have made us into perhaps the most uncertain and chaotic civilization. To be consciously in touch with inner life may help, not to restore certainty, but to foster an acknowledgment of the complexity inherent in interrelatedness. The stories in this book show that to exclude a vital source of inner knowing results in the experience of disharmony within the individual. The resulting lack of integration within must have consequences for an understanding of our relationship with society and nature. How can one perceive and foster relatedness and interdependence in the world if one suppresses it within oneself? The wisdom and experience of the centuries remind us that inner and outer are inseparable.

In our stories we tried hard, and at times in painful honesty, to bring body, emotion, and mind together, and in doing so, also self and other. We have described how problems we encountered in our work turned out to be problems of feeling and living as much as of thinking. But while we can talk about this in retrospect, at any given time the actual connectedness between body, emotion, mind, and action can only be felt, not thought.

"Feelings *are* the direct connections between actual occasions of experience," says Catherine Keller (1988, p. 183); "It is not just a matter of feeling the relations, but of feelings *as* relations." Feelings are what actualize the possible — anything rational or abstract is useful inasmuch as it gets concretely actualized in life, otherwise it cannot advance the realization of the visions it expresses (Keller, 1988, p. 211).

It may be that one of the most difficult aspects of embodying our work and our lives will involve giving up the idea that everything can be thought. The emerging epistemology that informs this book involves replacing the modern era's near-exclusive focus on reason and thought with a more natural integration of all ways of knowing. If we continue to try to rely exclusively on what can be expressed in thought and language, on rationality and abstraction in whatever contemporary postmodern voices they are expressed, we will continue to work in irrationalities. Rationality *removed* from other ways of knowing perpetrates the worst irrationalities (Keller, 1988, p. 178). We believe our stories attest to this.

Several things struck us as we read and reread the manuscript. While each individual story stands on its own, we were at the same time struck, as the contributions came in, by how they orchestrated themselves into collective messages. The focus across contributions was not on how to solve the problems of methodology, but how to deepen, problematize, and reorient them. This involved infusing inquiry with feeling, and with concerns for relatedness and justice, while questioning one's own place within conceptions of research and method. Why research? How to be in research? Who to be in research? These questions featured far more prominently than the method question: What to do in research? Research became increasingly apprehended as, in the first instance, a relation rather than an activity, a relation that acts *in* the world as distinct from a set of methodological practices that act *on* the world. All contributors expressed deep concern that we need to be in research in ways that do not violate the other, or ourselves. What we as editors take from this volume are serious concerns about the nature of the distance between self and other in research, a distance that veils many problems and that keeps disturbing our conscience.

We hope, then, that this book will give heart to those who wish to consciously harmonize thought, reason, and intellect with tacit, somatic, and other nonrational ways of knowing and who wish to blur the boundaries between self and other in research, but who face opposition from both the politics of research and the politics of their wider communities.

We need to distinguish, however, between harmonizing reason and feeling, the rational and the tacit, and a recent tendency within qualitative research to engage in beliefs opposite from those articulated by positivism, and which are therefore anchored in its same dualisms. Our concerns here regard the tendency to indulge the self of the researcher in practices that seem to resemble self-therapy, or that reflect humanist values focused on the researcher's desire for her/his own self-actualization, or that turn research studies into a practice of creativity for the sake of practicing creativity. We have encountered all of these, primarily through our involvement in thesis and dissertation committees. Now that the need to be objective, by trying to set aside all personal needs, has fallen away, the focus can easily turn to the opposite side of the paired constructs of objectivity/subjectivity, to a focus *on* the personal needs of the researcher. Others, too, have expressed concern about texts becoming "narcissistic and egotistical" (Bruner, in Denzin & Lincoln, 1994a, p. 578). Such focus on the personal needs of the researcher is distinct and different from the focus on the nonrational as a source of knowing.

As we face unprecedented problems for ourselves and the next generations, problems in part brought about, or exacerbated by, an excessive focus on the idea of the individual as a self-enclosed entity, social research is considering the major inadequacies inherent in such a focus, for it perpetuates the enlightenment project with its belief that the starting point for being, knowing, and action is founded on the primacy of the individual. What if we start from the premise that the starting point that forms the basis for being, knowing, and acting exists in a fundamental connectedness within larger life forms? Applying this to research, the binary images of "us" and "them," including the "researcher" on the one hand and "research participants" on the other, becomes problematic. How would one then have to rethink the very idea of research, and of "being a researcher"?

As noted in Chapter 1, the concepts of fundamental relatedness and of reenchantment have been used in relation to cultural and ideological analyses of the history of the world (Berman, 1984), to the nature of science (Bohm, 1980; Griffin, 1988), to the nature and function of art (Gablik, 1991), and to the nature of feminist thought (Keller, 1988; Waugh, 1989). Relatedness and reenchantment in these discussions is not about developing ways to achieve self-actualization, or creativity, or personal enlightenment. It is rather about the reentering of participatory relatedness. Ways of knowing through intimate relatedness and attention are "a mode of access," as Evelyn Fox Keller (1986, p. 175) refers to this knowing, "honored by time and human experience." It addresses a longing that one's life and work are of value to the socioecological needs of the whole because of the simple realization that we *are* those needs and we *are* that whole.

What we read in several contributions to this book is the wish for educational and social research to be so reenchanted, and even more pointedly, that research that emerges from and enters deeply into fundamental relatedness must be the key to the future. Postmechanistic and postpatriarchical conceptions of knowing involve the reimagining of the self, not just of the other. Reimagining the other we do all the time. Reimagining the self-enclosed self of the enlightenment project into larger, participatory realities is far more difficult because it demands a letting go of the notion of the separative self as a starting point for knowing. Perhaps that is one of the more important threads within the tapestry of our stories: They speak to the difficulties involved in reimagining the self-enclosed self.

The above comments on separateness versus connectedness in research have meaning particularly within the heritage of mainstream Western thought, which tends to see life in binary and oppositional terms, taking the idea of a separate self as the basis for theories of rationality. In terms of connectedness we think of examples of indigenous people's research in which both the researcher and those he or she works with are not seen as separate individuals, nor as separate starting points for constructing knowledge. Rather, the collective nature of life is the starting point and the focus of concern. Russell Bishop (1995), for instance, used the term *whakawhanaungatanga*, which literally means establishing relationships in a Maori context, to describe a research process within a Maori worldview of collaboratively constructing research in a "culturally conscious and connected manner" (p. 224). Relatedness was the fundamental and ongoing basis of everything that occurred in the research project, and researchers understood themselves to be involved "somatically in the research process; that is physically, ethically, morally and spiritually" (p. 232). This is to speak of much more than "establishing rapport," of more than co-planning or co-authoring. Oppression is acknowledged by all as a material reality, but the notion of "a researcher" working with "subjugated voices," for instance, does not characterize the research relationship. The researchers as persons were essentially indistinguishable from the researchers as researchers. The collective nature of life was both the starting point and the focus of the research; individuals are strands in this web that exists as history, ancestry, the present, and the future.

Reimagining the self into such larger realities may lead to a core question that we believe the collective contributions in this volume raise: What, then, is the difference between doing research and knowing as a researcher on the one hand, and knowing as a nonresearcher on the other hand, but for the pragmatics of being afforded time, resources, and getting paid to engage in articulating and questioning knowledge? What kind of reimagining of the self is needed to answer this question? None of the contributors has phrased it this way, but as we read and reread the manuscript, this question seemed to stare at us from between the lines in several cases. Can we continue to use the label "researcher" to refer to ourselves without calling up in those who are the focus of our research, in those with whom we collaboratively engage in research, in the readers of our publications, and, not in the least, in ourselves, just that ego-flattering lingering hint of privileged knowing, or of privileged status—whether we are conscious of it or not—that sets us outside of community, of otherself interrelatedness?

This seems to us a most central question, and we have just begun to face it in ourselves. It is also a question that is hard to ask. Even publications that "work" the "hyphens" between self and other in qualitative research, as Michelle Fine (1994) does so incisively, addressing the "colonizing discourse"—and therefore the colonizing self–other relationship that colors much of qualitative research—stop short of questioning whether referring to oneself as researcher is not a colonizing act in itself. "Residues of domination linger heavily within these qualitative texts," concludes Fine (1994, p. 81), referring to the work of "activist researchers" working with "subjugated voices." These studies, too, Fine says, will in time become a "contested site." But Fine also still believes that one can, in fact, be a "researcher."

We need a fresh definition and a reimagination and articulation of what being a researcher means in postprivileged ways of knowing if we are to continue to refer to ourselves in this way, as most likely we will. In discussing this between ourselves, we acknowledged that when someone asks us what we do in our jobs, we become uncomfortable. We say, I teach—or work—at the university. When asked, Do you do research? or Do you have to do research? (as the question is not infrequently phrased), we mumble something about liking to study and to write. We don't mumble because we think that what we do has no value, but because we are suspicious of the demands of the ego involved when saying, I am a researcher. To say so makes us stand out and feel separate in a way we no longer wish to stand out and be separated. It makes us feel as if we wrap a cloak of mystery and pretense around ourselves. What, then, can it still mean to say, I am a researcher?

In restoring a participatory and embodied understanding of what is involved in constructing knowledge, we might perhaps think of research as a responsiveness to the integrity of life forms beyond the self. Such nonegocentric responsiveness as a characterization of research is emerging, we think, from the work, for instance, of Hillary Rose (1994) and Mary Catherine Keller (1988). Gregory Bateson (1972) and Mary Catherine Bateson (1977) speak explicitly of love and wisdom to characterize both knowing the self as interwoven within larger realities, and to knowing larger realities as part of self. Rose (1994) calls her book *Love, Power and Knowledge.* "It is love, as caring respect for both people and nature, that offers an ethic to reshape knowledge, and with it society," she says (Rose, 1994, p. 238). As noted in Chapter 1, Evelyn Fox Keller (1983) records Barbara McClintock's vocabulary of affection, love, and intimacy when she spoke of her scientific work and of the need to "forget yourself" (in Keller, 1983, p. 117) in order to access a larger reality. In this context knowing as nonegocentric responsiveness, as love, care, and intimacy, does not refer to psychological needs, but to an awareness of kinship and thus to the selfother unity that characterizes kinship.[1] It becomes an ontological and epistemological equation, rather than a psychological one.

The equation of knowing by separate selves as a process of distancing, mastery, and conquest has dominated our lives for centuries. Living toward knowing as a nonegocentric responsiveness that takes as its starting point kinship and identification is at once a most hopeful and urgent development. For this to materialize, scholarship needs to develop a language that, as Patricia Williams (1991, p. 62) says, "encourages looking at others as part of ourselves." It needs to attend, in Toni Morrison's (1992, p. 4) words, to what makes possible "this process of entering what one is estranged from." Given the intricate relatedness of intellectual, somatic, and emotive life, such development cannot but include all ways of knowing.

Note

1. Positing selfother unity as the primary starting point for scholarship also suggests ecological (Bateson, 1972; Evernden, 1985; Livingston, 1994) and certain feminist sensibilities (Gablik, 1991; Keller, 1988; Waugh, 1989). It further points to an integration of Eastern and Western thought (Kalamaras, 1994; Varela, Thompson, & Rosch, 1993). The Western humanist, essentialist, and patriarchical self-enclosed subject is gone, an erasure announced in postmodern deconstructionism as "The Death of the Self" (Kalamaras, 1994, p. 201). For some, says Foster (in Waugh, 1989, p. 2), this death is a great loss, " . . . and may lead to narcissistic laments about the end of art, of culture, of the west. But for others, precisely for Others, this is no great loss at all." The ecological, feminist, and East–West sensibilities referred to above go further than the deconstructionist rejection of and opposition to the modernist construct of the self, and at least open up the possibility for the *re*-construction of a self *in and through* relatedness, and for nonegocentric responsiveness in knowledge construction.

References

Alther, L. (1990). *Bedrock*. London: Penguin.

Anderson, W. T. (1990). *Reality isn't what it used to be: Theatrical politics, ready-to-wear religion, global myths, primitive chic, and other wonders of the postmodern world*. New York: Harper & Row.

Anglin, J. P. (1988). The parent networks project: Towards a collaborative methodology for ecological research. In A. R. Pence (Ed.), *Ecological research with families and children: From concepts to methods* (pp. 35–48). New York: Teachers College Press.

Arnold, J. C. (1995). *Alcohol and the chosen few: Organizational reproduction in an addictive system*. Unpublished doctoral dissertation, Indiana University, Bloomington, IN.

Aronowitz, S. (1988). *Science as power: Discourse and ideology in modern society*. Minneapolis: University of Minnesota Press.

Atkin, K. (1991). Health, illness, disability and black minorities: A speculative critique of present day discourse. *Disability, Handicap and Society, 6*(1), 37–47.

Baldwin, J. (1961). *Nobody knows my name*. New York: Dell.

Ballard, K. (1987). The limitations of behavioural approaches to teaching: Some implications for special education. *The Exceptional Child, 34*, 197–212.

Ballard, K. (Ed.). (1994). *Disability, family, whanau and society*. Palmerston North, New Zealand: Dunmore Press.

Ballard, K. (1995). Inclusion, paradigms, power and participation. In C. Clark, A. Dyson, & A. Millward (Eds.), *Towards inclusive schools?* (pp. 1–14). London: David Folton.

Ballard, K., Watson, M., Bray, A., Burrows, L., & MacArthur, J. (1992). *The Otago Family Network: A report on the research contract to the Research and Statistics Division, Ministry of Education*. Dunedin, New Zealand: Donald Beasley Institute and University of Otago.

Barker, F. (1984). *The tremulous private body: Essays on subjection*. New York: Methuen.

Bartlett, D. L., & Steele, J. B. (1992). *America: What went wrong?* Kansas City, MO: Andrews & McMeel.

Bateson, G. (1972). *Steps to an ecology of mind*. New York: Chandler.

Bateson, M. C. (1977). Daddy, can a scientist be wise? In J. Brockman (Ed.), *About Bateson* (pp. 56–73). New York: Dutton.

F., Clinchy, B. M., Goldberger, N. R., & Tarule, J. M. (1986). *n's ways of knowing: The development of self, voice, and mind.* New Basic Books.

N., Madsen, R., Sullivan, W. M., Swidler, A., & Tipton, S. M. 1). *The good society.* New York: Alfred A. Knopf.

Ðɛ_{ᴵᴸ}. M. (1984). *The reenchantment of the world.* New York: Bantam.

Berman, M. (1989). *Coming to our senses: Body and spirit in the hidden history of the West.* New York: Bantam.

Bernstein, R. (1983). *Beyond objectivity and relativism.* Philadelphia: University of Pennsylvania Press.

Bishop, R. (1995). *Collaborative research stories: Whakawhanaungatanga.* Unpublished doctoral dissertation, University of Otago, New Zealand.

Bishop, R., & Glynn, T. (1992, November). *Participant driven empowering research: Issues arising in a bicultural context.* Paper presented at the Australia Association for Research in Education/New Zealand Association for Research in Education Joint Conference, Deakin University, Geelong, Australia.

Bloom, L. R. (1993). *"Shot through with streams of songs": Explorations of interpretive research methodology.* Unpublished doctoral dissertation, Indiana University, Bloomington.

Bohm, D. (1980). *Wholeness and the implicate order.* Boston: Routledge & Kegan Paul.

Bohm, D. (1984). Insight, knowledge, science and human values. In D. Sloan (Ed.), *Toward the recovery of wholeness: Knowledge, education, and human values* (pp. 8–30). New York: Teachers College Press.

Bordo, S. R. (1986). The Cartesian masculinization of thought. *Signs: Journal of Women in Culture and Society, 11*(3), 439–456.

Bordo, S. R. (1987). *The flight to objectivity: Essays on cartesianism and culture.* Albany: State University of New York Press.

Bowers, C. (1993). *Critical essays on education, modernity, and the recovery of the ecological imperative.* New York: Teachers College Press.

Britzman, D. (1991). *Practice makes practice.* Albany: State University of New York Press.

Bronfenbrenner, U. (1979). *The ecology of human development: Experiments by nature and design.* Cambridge, MA: Harvard University Press.

Bruner, J. (1985). Narrative and paradigmatic modes of thought. In E. Eisner (Ed.), *Learning and teaching the ways of knowing* (pp. 97–115) (Eighty-fourth Yearbook of the National Society for the Study of Education, Part 11). Chicago: University of Chicago Press.

Bruner, J. (1987). Life as narrative. *Social Research, 54*(1), 11–32.

Burke, J. (1985). *The day the universe changed.* Boston: Little, Brown.

Campbell, D. T., & Stanley, J. C. (1966). *Experimental and quasi-experimental designs for research.* Chicago: Rand McNally.

Carr, W., & Kemmis, S. (1986). *Becoming critical: Education, knowledge and action research.* London: Falmer Press.

Clandinin, D. J., & Connelly, F. M. (1991). Narrative and story in practice and research. In D. A. Schön (Ed.), *The reflective turn: Case studies in and on educational practice* (pp. 258–281). New York: Teachers College Press.

Coles, R. (1989). *The call of stories.* Boston: Houghton Mifflin.

Coles, R. (1990). *The spiritual life of children.* Boston: Houghton Mifflin.

Cook, T., & Campbell, D. (1979). *Quasi-experimentation: Design and analysis for field settings.* Boston: Houghton Mifflin.

Crowell, S. (1989). A new way of thinking: The challenge of the future. *Educational Leadership, 47*(1), 60–63.

Crown, L. (1990). *Children's voices.* Unpublished paper, York University Faculty of Education, North York, Ontario, Canada.

Daly, M. (1973). *Beyond God the Father.* Boston: Beacon Press.

Davies, P., & Gribbin, J. (1992). *The matter myth.* New York: Simon & Schuster.

Denzin, N. K., & Lincoln, Y. S. (Eds.). (1994a). *Handbook of qualitative research.* Newbury Park, CA: Sage.

Denzin, N. K., & Lincoln, Y. S. (1994b). Introduction: Entering the field of qualitative research. In N. K. Denzin & Y. S. Lincoln (Eds.), *Handbook of qualitative research* (pp. 1–18). Newbury Park, CA: Sage.

Dewey, J. (1929). *Experience and nature.* London: Allen & Unwin.

Dewey, J. (1960). *The quest for certainty: A study of the relation of knowledge and action.* New York: Capricorn Books.

Doll, W. E. (1986). Prigogine: A new sense of order, a new curriculum. *Theory Into Practice, 25*(1), 10–16.

Doll, W. E. (1993). *A post-modern perspective on curriculum.* New York: Teachers College Press.

Donaldson, M. (1992). *Human minds: An exploration.* London: Penguin.

Donmoyer, R. (1990). Generalizability and the single-case study. In E. Eisner & A. Peshkin (Eds.), *Qualitative inquiry in education: The continuing debate* (pp. 175–200). New York: Teachers College Press.

Duckworth, E. (1987). *"The having of wonderful ideas" and other essays on teaching and learning.* New York: Teachers College Press.

Edelsky, C. (1990). Whose agenda is this anyway? A response to McKenna, Robinson, and Miller. *Educational Researcher, 19*(8), 7–11.

Edgerton, R. B. (1967). *The cloak of competence: Stigma in the lives of the mentally retarded.* Berkeley: University of California Press.

Eisner, E. W. (1993). Forms of understanding and the future of educational research. *Educational Researcher, 22*(7), 5–11.

Eisner, E. W., & Peshkin, A. (Eds.). (1990). *Qualitative inquiry in education: The continuing debate.* New York: Teachers College Press.

Ellis, C., & Flaherty, M. G. (Eds.). (1992). *Investigating subjectivity: Research on lived experience.* Newbury Park, CA: Sage.

Ellsworth, E. (1989). Why doesn't this feel empowering? Working through the repressive myths of critical pedagogy. *Harvard Educational Review, 59,* 297–324.

Erickson, F. (1994, February). *I was in the bottom reading group: Ethnography, biography, and autobiography.* Paper presented at the annual Ethnography in Education Research Forum, Philadelphia, PA.

180   References

Evernden, N. (1985). *The natural alien: Humankind and environment*. Toronto: University of Toronto Press.

Fine, M. (1994). Working the hyphens: Reinventing self and other in qualitative research. In N. K. Denzin & Y. S. Lincoln (Eds.), *Handbook of qualitative research* (pp. 70–82). Newbury Park, CA: Sage.

Fontana, A., & Frey, J. H. (1994). Interviewing: The art of science. In N. K. Denzin & Y. S. Lincoln (Eds.), *Handbook of qualitative research* (pp. 361–376). Newbury Park, CA: Sage.

Fromm, E. (1964). *Escape from freedom*. New York: Holt, Rinehart, & Winston.

Frye, N. (Ed.). (1966). *Blake: A collection of critical essays*. Englewood Cliffs, NJ: Prentice-Hall.

Fulcher, G. (1989). *Disabling policies? A comparative approach to education policy and disability*. Bristol, PA: Falmer Press.

Gablik, S. (1991). *The re-enchantment of art*. New York: Thames & Hudson.

Gadamer, H. G. (1975). *Truth and method* (G. Barden & J. Cumming, Eds. & Trans.). New York: Seabury Press.

Gee, J. P. (1990). *Social linguistics and literacies: Ideology in discourses*. Bristol, PA: Falmer Press.

Geertz, C. (1988). *Works and lives: The anthropologist as author*. Stanford: Stanford University Press.

Giddens, A. (1976). *New rules of the sociological method*. New York: Basic Books.

Goodman, J. (1992). Theoretical and practical considerations for school based research in a post-positivist era. *Qualitative Studies in Education, 5*(2), 117–133.

Gordimer, N. (1990). *My son's story*. London: Bloomsbury.

Gould, S. J. (1981). *The mismeasure of man*. Harmondsworth: Penguin.

Graves, D. H. (1984). *A researcher learns to write*. Exeter, NH: Heinemann.

Griffin, D. R. (Ed.). (1988). *The reenchantment of science*. Albany: State University of New York Press.

Griffin, S. (1984). Split culture. In S. Kuman (Ed.), *The Schumacher Series. Volume II*. London: Blond & Briggs.

Grumet, M. (1991). The politics of personal knowledge. In C. Witherell & N. Noddings (Eds.), *Stories lives tell* (pp. 67–77). New York: Teachers College Press.

Guba, E. G. (1978). *Toward a methodology of naturalistic inquiry in educational evaluation* (CSE Monograph Series in Evaluation No. 8). Los Angeles: University of California, Center for the Study of Evaluation.

Guba, E. G. (Ed.). (1990). *The paradigm dialog*. Newbury Park, CA: Sage.

Harman, W. W. (1988). The need for restructuring of science. *Revisions, 11*(12), 13–21.

Havel, V. (1992a). The end of the modern era. *The New York Times*, Op-Ed, March 1.

Havel, V. (1992b). *Summer meditations*. New York: Alfred A. Knopf.

Hazelrigg, L. (1989). *Claims of knowledge.* Tallahassee: The Florida State University Press.

Herrnstein, R. J., & Murray, C. A. (1994). *The bell curve: Intelligence and class structure in American life.* New York: Free Press.

Heshusius, L. (1984). Why would they and I want to do it? A phenomenological-theoretical view of special education. *Learning Disability Quarterly, 7*(4), 363–368.

Heshusius, L. (1989). The Newtonian mechanistic paradigm, special education, and contours of alternatives: An overview. *Journal of Learning Disabilities, 22*(7), 402–415.

Heshusius, L. (1994). Freeing ourselves from objectivity: Managing subjectivity, or turning toward a participatory mode of consciousness? *Educational Researcher, 23*(3), 15–22.

Heshusius, L. (1995). Holism and special education: There is no substitute for real life purposes and processes. In T. M. Skrtic (Ed.), *Disability and democracy: Reconstructing (special) education for postmodernity* (pp. 166–189). New York: Teachers College Press.

Hillesum, E. (1983). *An interrupted life: The diaries of Etty Hillesum.* New York: Washington Square Press.

Honan, W. H. (1994, August). Ode to academic nastiness. *New York Times* [Education Life], p. 38.

hooks, b. (1989). *Talking back: Thinking feminist, thinking black.* Boston, MA: South End Press.

hooks, b. (1990). *Yearning: Race, gender and cultural politics.* New York: between the lines.

Hunter, A. (Ed.). (1990). *The rhetoric of social research.* New Brunswick, NJ: Rutgers University Press.

Jackson, B., & Marsden, D. (1962). *Education and the working class.* London: Routledge & Kegan Paul.

Jackson, M. (1989). *Paths toward a clearing.* Bloomington: Indiana University Press.

Jackson, P. (1968). *Life in classrooms.* New York: Holt, Rinehart, & Winston.

Jagger, A. M. (1989). Love and knowledge: Emotion in feminist epistemology. In A. M. Jagger & S. R. Bordo (Eds.), *Gender/Body/Knowledge: Feminist reconstructions of being and knowing* (pp. 145–171). New Brunswick, NJ: Rutgers University Press.

Jagger, A. M., & Bordo, S. R. (Eds.). (1989). *Gender/Body/Knowledge: Feminist reconstructions of being and knowing.* New Brunswick, NJ: Rutgers University Press.

Johnson, D. (1983). *Body.* Boston: Beacon Press.

Jung, C. (1933). *Modern man in search of a soul.* New York: Harcourt Brace Jovanovich.

Kalamaras, G. (1994). *Reclaiming the tacit dimension: Symbolic form in the rhetoric of silence.* Albany: State University of New York Press.

Kavanaugh, K., & Rodriguez, O. (Trans.). (1991). *The collected works of St. John of the Cross.* Washington, DC: Institute for Carmelite Studies.

Keen, S. (1990). *To a dancing god.* San Francisco: Harper & Row.

Keller, C. (1988). *From a broken web: Separation, sexism, and self.* Boston: Beacon Press.

Keller, E. F. (1983). *A feeling for the organism.* San Francisco: W. H. Freeman.

Keller, E. F. (1985). *Reflections on gender and science.* New Haven: Yale University Press.

Keller, E. F. (1986). How gender matters, or, Why it's so hard for us to count past two. In J. Harding (Ed.), *Perspectives on gender and science* (pp. 168–183). London: Falmer Press.

Kelly, G. A. (1955). *The psychology of personal constructs* (Vols. 1 & 2). New York: W. W. Norton.

Kesson, K. (1991). The unfinished puzzle: Sustaining a dynamic holism. *Holistic Education Review, 4*(4), 44–49.

Kitzinger, C. (1990). The rhetoric of pseudoscience. In I. Parker & J. Shotter (Eds.), *Deconstructing social psychology* (pp. 61–75). London: Sage.

Kremer, J. (1992). The dark night of the scholar: Reflections on culture and ways of knowing. *Revision: The Journal of Change in Consciousness, 14*(4), 169–178.

Krieger, S. (1991). *Social science and the self: Personal essays on an art form.* New Brunswick, NJ: Rutgers University Press.

Krishnamurti, J. (1954). *The first and last freedom.* New York: Harper & Row.

Krishnamurti, J. (1972). *You are the world.* New York: Harper & Row.

Kubrin, D. (1981). Newton's inside out! Magic, class struggle, and the rise of mechanism in the West. In H. Woolf (Ed.), *The analytic spirit: Essays in the history of science* (pp. 96–121). Ithaca, NY: Cornell University Press.

Kuhn, T. S. (1970). *The structure of scientific revolutions.* Chicago: University of Chicago Press.

Kyle, J., & Pullen, G. (1988). Culture in contact: Deaf and hearing people. *Disability, Handicap and Society, 3,* 49–61.

Laing, R. D. (1972). *The politics of the family and other essays.* New York: Vintage Books.

Larsen, S., & Poplin, M. S. (1980). *Methods for educating the handicapped: An individualized education program approach.* Boston: Allyn & Bacon.

Lather, P. (1991). Deconstructing/deconstructive inquiry: The politics of knowing and being known. *Educational Theory, 41*(2), 153–173.

Lincoln, Y. S., & Guba, E. G. (1985). *Naturalistic inquiry.* Beverly Hills, CA: Sage.

Livingston, J. A. (1994). *Rogue primate: An exploration of human domestication.* Toronto: Porter Books.

McDonald, J. P. (1992). *Teaching: Making sense of an uncertain craft.* New York: Teachers College Press.

Magolda, P. M. (1994). *A quest for community: An ethnographic study of a residential college.* Unpublished doctoral dissertation, Indiana University, Bloomington.

Melamed, E. (1985). *Play and playfulness in women's learning and development*. Unpublished doctoral dissertation, University of Toronto, Canada.

Mezirow, J. (1990). *Fostering critical reflection in adulthood: A guide to transformative and emancipatory learning*. San Francisco: Jossey-Bass.

Miles, M. B., & Huberman, A. M. (1984). *Qualitative data analysis: A sourcebook of new methods*. Beverly Hills, CA: Sage.

Miller, J. P. (1988). *The holistic curriculum*. Toronto: The Ontario Institute for Studies in Education Press.

Miller, R. (1990). *What are schools for? Holistic education in American culture*. Brandan, VT: Holistic Education Press.

Morrison, T. (1992). *Playing in the dark: Whiteness and the literary imagination*. Cambridge, MA: Harvard University Press.

Myers, I. B. (1980). *Gifts differing*. Palo Alto, CA: Consulting Psychologists Press.

Nielsen, J. M. (1990). Introduction. In J. M. Nielsen (Ed.), *Feminist research methods: Exemplary readings in the social sciences* (pp. 1–37). Boulder, CO: Westview Press.

Noddings, N. (1986). Fidelity in teaching, teacher education, and research for teaching. *Harvard Educational Review, 56*(2), 502–512.

Noddings, N. (1988). An ethic of care and its implications for instructional arrangements. *American Journal of Education, 96*(2), 223–231.

Noddings, N. (1991). Stories in dialogue: Caring and interpersonal reasoning. In C. Witherell & N. Noddings (Eds.), *Stories lives tell* (pp. 157–170). New York: Teachers College Press.

Nussbaum, M. (1990). *Love's knowledge: Essays on philosophy and literature*. New York: Oxford University Press.

O'Brien, M. (1990). Political ideology and patriarchal education. In F. Forman (Ed.), *Feminism and education* (pp. 3–26). Toronto: OISE Press.

Okri, B. (1993). *Songs of enchantment*. London: Jonathan Cape.

Oldfather, P. (1991). *Students' perceptions of their own reasons/purposes for being or not being involved in learning activities: A qualitative study of student motivation*. Unpublished doctoral dissertation, Claremont Graduate School, Department of Education, Claremont, California.

Oliver, D., & Gershman, K. W. (1989). *Education, modernity, and fractured meaning: Toward a process theory of teaching and learning*. Albany: State University of New York Press.

Oliver, M. (1992). Changing the social relations of research production? *Disability, Handicap and Society, 7*(2), 101–114.

Ondaatje, M. (1992). *The English patient*. London: Bloomsbury.

Owen, H. (1987). *Spirit: Transformation and development in organizations*. Potomac, MD: Abbott Publishing.

Owen, H. (1990). *Leadership is*. Potomac, MD: Abbott Publishing.

Owen, H. (1991). *Riding the tiger: Doing business in a transforming world*. Potomac, MD: Abbott Publishing.

Piaget, J. (1986). *The construction of reality in the child*. New York: International Universities Press.

Polanyi, M. (1966). *The tacit dimension*. London: Routledge & Kegan.

Polkinghorne, D. (1988). *Narrative knowing and the human sciences*. Albany: State University of New York Press.

Poplin, M. S. (1987). Self-imposed blindness: The scientific method in education. *Remedial and Special Education, 8*(6), 31–37.

Poplin, M. S. (1988). The reductionistic fallacy in learning disabilities: Replicating the past by reducing the present. *Journal of Learning Disabilities, 21*(7), 389–400.

Poplin, M., & Weeres, J. (1992). *Voices from the inside: A report on schooling from inside the classroom*. Claremont, CA: The Institute for Education in Transformation.

Popper, K. (1986). *The poverty of historicism*. London: Ark Publishing.

Prigogine, I., & Stengers, I. (1984). *Order out of chaos: Man's new dialogue with nature*. New York: Bantam.

Putnam, H. (1981). *Reason, truth, and history*. Cambridge, England: Cambridge University Press.

Reinharz, S. (1979). *On becoming a social scientist*. San Francisco: Jossey-Bass.

Reinharz, S. (1992). *Feminist methods in social research*. New York: Oxford University Press.

Rhodes, W. (1975). *A study of child variance. Vol. 4: The future*. Ann Arbor: University of Michigan Publications Distribution Service.

Rhodes, W. (1987). Ecology and the new physics. *Behavior Disorders, 13*(1), 58–61.

Rhodes, W., & Head, S. (1974). *A study of child variance. Vol. 3: Service delivery systems*. Ann Arbor: University of Michigan Press.

Rhodes, W., & Tracy, M. (Eds.). (1974a). *A study of child variance. Vol. 1: Conceptual model*. Ann Arbor: University of Michigan Press.

Rhodes, W., & Tracy, M. (Eds.). (1974b). *A study of child variance. Vol. 2: Interventions*. Ann Arbor: University of Michigan Press.

Richardson, R. D. (1990). *Ralph Waldo Emerson: Selected essays, lectures, and poems*. New York: Bantam.

Rist, R. (1973). *The urban school: Factory for failure*. Cambridge, MA: MIT Press.

Rivera, J. (1992). *Aftermath: The police, Rodney King, Martin Luther King, and education—How does it all add up?* Washington, DC: The American Council on Education.

Rorty, R. (1979). *Philosophy and the mirror of nature*. Princeton, NJ: Princeton University Press.

Rorty, R. (1982). Method, social science and social hope. In R. Rorty (Ed.), *Consequences of pragmatism* (pp. 191–229). Minneapolis: University of Minnesota Press.

Rose, H. (1994). *Love, power and knowledge: Toward a feminist transformation of the sciences*. Bloomington: Indiana University Press.

Rothfield, P. (1990). Feminism, subjectivity, and sexual difference. In S. Gunew (Ed.), *Feminist knowledge: Critique and construct* (pp. 121–144). London: Routledge.

Rushdie, S. (1990). "Is Nothing Sacred?" *Granta, 31*, 97–111.

Saleebey, D. (1992). Biology's challenge to social work: Embodying the person-in-environment perspective. *Social Work, 37*(2), 112–118.

Saleebey, D., & Weick, A. (1994). *Restoring the body in social work practice and theory.* Unpublished paper. School of Social Welfare, University of Kansas.

Saul, J. R. (1992). *Voltaire's bastards: The dictatorship of reason in the West.* New York: Penguin.

Sawada, D., & Caley, M. T. (1985). Dissipative structures: New metaphors for becoming in education. *Educational Researcher, 14*(3), 13–25.

Schachtel, E. G. (1959). *Metamorphosis: On the development of affect, perception, attention and memory.* New York: Basic Books.

Schön, D. A. (1991). Concluding comments. In D. A. Schön (Ed.), *The reflective turn: Case studies in and out of educational practice* (pp. 343–359). New York: Teachers College Press.

Shannon, P. (1988). *Broken promises: Reading instruction in the 20th century.* Granby, MA: Bergin & Garvey.

Skrtic, T. M. (1991). *Behind special education: A critical analysis of professional culture and school organization.* Denver: Love Publishing.

Sloan, D. (Ed.). (1984). *Toward the recovery of wholeness: Knowledge, education, and human values.* New York: Teachers College Press.

Smith, J. K. (1989). *The nature of social and educational inquiry: Empiricism versus interpretation.* Norwood, NJ: Ablex.

Smith, J. K. (1993). *After the demise of empiricism: The problem of judging social and educational inquiry.* Norwood, NJ: Ablex.

Smith, J. K., & Heshusius, L. (1986). Closing down the conversation: The end of the quantitative–qualitative debate among educational inquirers. *Educational Researcher, 15*(1), 4–12.

Smith, P. (1990). *Killing the spirit: Higher education in America.* New York: Penguin.

Spretnik, C. (1991). *States of grace: The recovery of meaning in the postmodern age.* San Francisco: Harper.

Tarnas, R. (1991). *The passion of the Western mind.* New York: Ballantine Books.

Taylor, D. (1994, May). *The ideologies and ethics of family literacy pedagogies: A postformal perspective.* Paper presented at the annual meeting of the International Reading Association, Toronto, Ontario, Canada.

Varela, F. J., Thompson, E., & Rosch, E. (1993). *The embodied mind: Cognitive science and human experience.* New York: MIT Press.

Vygotsky, L. (1987). *Thought and language.* Cambridge: MIT Press.

Walker, M. U. (1992). Moral understandings: Alternative "epistemology" for a feminist ethics. In E. B. Cole & S. Coultrap-McQuin (Eds.), *Explorations in feminist ethics* (pp. 166–168). Bloomington: Indiana University Press.

Walker, R. (1990). *Ka whawhai tonu matou: Struggle without end.* Auckland, New Zealand: Penguin.

Waller, W. (1932). *Sociology of teaching.* New York: Wiley.

Walsh, J. P. (1995). *Knowledge of angels*. London: Black Swan.

Waugh, P. (1989). *Feminine fictions: Revisiting the postmodern*. New York: Routledge.

Webster's New World Dictionary, College Edition. (1960). New York: World Publishing Co.

Westbrook, R. B. (1991). *John Dewey and American democracy*. Ithaca, NY: Cornell University Press.

Westkott, M. (1979). Feminist criticism of the social sciences. *Harvard Educational Review, 49*(4), 422–430.

Whitehead, A. N. (1953[1925]). *Science and the modern world*. New York: Macmillan.

Whyte, W. F. (1955). *Street corner society: The social structure of an Italian slum*. Chicago: University of Chicago Press.

Williams, P. T. (1991). *The alchemy of race and rights: Diary of a law professor*. Cambridge: Harvard University Press.

Wilshire, B. (1990). *The moral collapse of the university*. Albany: State University of New York Press.

Witherell, C., & Noddings, N. (Eds.). (1991). *Stories lives tell: Narrative and dialogue in education*. New York: Teachers College Press.

Woolf, V. (1931). *The waves*. London: Hogarth Press.

About the Contributors

James P. Anglin is an Associate Professor at the School of Child and Youth Care, University of Victoria, British Columbia, Canada. He teaches the fundamentals of change at the undergraduate level and graduate seminars in professional and organizational development. He co-edited *Perspectives in Professional Child and Youth Care* and is on the editorial boards of the *Journal of Child and Youth Care, Child and Youth Care Forum*, and the *Journal of Emotional and Behavioral Problems*. His current research relates to capacity building for family life and residential group care for young people.

Keith Ballard is an Associate Professor of Education at the University of Otago, Dunedin, New Zealand. His earlier work includes publications in the *Journal of Applied Behavior Analysis, Journal of Abnormal Child Psychology*, and *Child and Family Behavior Therapy*. More recently, his writing has involved papers and monographs exploring a sociopolitical analysis of disability issues, and includes the book *Disability, Family, Whanau and Society*, written in collaboration with parents of disabled children.

Curt Dudley-Marling taught at the University of Colorado at Denver before taking up his present position as Professor of Education at York University, Toronto, Canada. His work focuses mainly on language and literacy with struggling readers and writers. He has written *Readers and Writers with a Difference, When School Is a Struggle, When Students Have Time to Talk*, and *Who Owns Learning?* He recently took leave from his university duties to teach third grade in a Toronto-area school.

Deborah J. Gallagher is an Assistant Professor of Special Education at the University of Northern Iowa. After nine years of classroom experience in the public schools, she now teaches undergraduate and graduate courses in the area of learning disabilities. Her recent publications have appeared in journals such as *Case in Point* and *Qualitative Studies in Education*. She is also co-author of a book entitled *Managing Classroom Behavior: A Reflective Case-Based Approach*.

Egon G. Guba is Professor Emeritus of Education at Indiana University, Bloomington, where for a time he served as Associate Dean of the School of Education, and is currently Adjunct Professor of Educational Administration at Texas A & M University. He earlier served at the University of Chicago and Ohio State University, where he directed the Bureau of Educational Research and Service. Until his retirement he taught evaluation and inquiry methodology, with an emphasis on qualitative methods. With his colleague and spouse, Yvonna S. Lincoln, he has written numerous articles and several books, including *Effective Evaluation, Naturalistic Inquiry*, and, most recently, *Fourth Generation Evaluation*.

Lous Heshusius is a Professor of Education at York University, Toronto. Her work has focused on paradigmatic critiques of special education and on qualitative thought, reflecting questions of ideological, gendered, and cultural ways of knowing. Her articles have appeared in journals such as *Exceptional Children, Educational Researcher*, and the *Journal of Learning Disabilities*. She has published a participant observation study, *Meaning in Life*, from the perspective of those labeled retarded, and *Portraits*, a translation of an award-winning Dutch series of prose pictures of marginalized people by Lize Stilma.

Neita Kay Israelite is an Associate Professor of Education at York University, Toronto, Canada. Her areas of interest are education and rehabilitation of people who are deaf and hard of hearing. Her earlier work focused on quantitative research on educational and psychological aspects of deafness. More recently, she has been using qualitative research strategies to understand the meanings that people construct from the experience of hearing loss. Her articles have appeared in the *American Annals of the Deaf* and *The Volta Review*.

Mary Simpson Poplin is a Professor of Education and Director of the Teacher Education Program and of the Institute for Education in Transformation at the Claremont Graduate School, Claremont, California. Her earlier work focused on special education and has extended to include linguistic differences, racism, qualitative inquiry, and spirituality in education. She has authored many articles and was the editor of *Learning Disability Quarterly*. She co-authored the national research report *Voices from the Inside: A Report on Schooling from Inside the Classroom*, which has sold over 50,000 copies since its publication in 1992.

William C. Rhodes is Distinguished Visiting Professor, Special Education at the University of South Florida, and Professor Emeritus of Education and Psychology at the University of Michigan. He has been Director of the State Mental Health Program in Georgia; Professor and Director of the Child Study Center at Peabody-Vanderbilt University; and Associate Director of Community Child Study Programs at the National Institute of Mental Health. At the present time he mentors and supervises research projects of participants in the William C. Rhodes Collegium in Postmodern Research. Among his many publications are six volumes of *A Study in Child Variance*.

Thomas A. Schwandt is an Associate Professor of Education at Indiana University, Bloomington. He teaches courses in qualitative methodology, philosophical foundations of social science inquiry, and theory of program evaluation. He is also a Fellow of the Poynter Center for the Study of Ethics and American Institutions at Indiana University. Papers addressing his interest in reuniting cognitive and moral concerns in social inquiry have appeared in *Educational Researcher, The Journal of Contemporary Ethnography, Evaluation Practice*, and in *The Quest for Quality*, edited by Birgitta Qvarsell and Bert L. T. van der Linden. His views on the foundations of interpretivist commitments in social inquiry were recently published in *The Handbook of Qualitative Research*.

John K. Smith is a Professor of Education at the University of Northern Iowa. He teaches courses in the areas of sociology of education and qualitative inquiry. His publications, which have focused on the philosophy of inquiry, have appeared in various journals, such as the *Educational Researcher*, the *Journal of Educational Administration*, and *Educational Evaluation and Policy Analysis*. He also has published two books: *The Nature of Social and Educational Inquiry* and *After the Demise of Empiricism*.

Index